$5.95

he U.S. and Israel 1945 - 1973

A Diplomatic History

By
Herbert Druks, Ph.D.

OVERDUE FINES ARE 25¢ PER DAY
PER ITEM

Return to book drop to remove
this checkout from your record.

Other books by Herbert Druks

Harry S Truman and the Russians, 1945 - 1953.
From Truman through Johnson (Two volumes).
The City in Western Civilization, Volume I.
The Failure to Rescue.

The U.S. and Israel
1945 - 1973

By
Herbert Druks, Ph.D.

Robert Speller & Sons, Publishers, Inc.
New York, New York 10010

© 1979 by Herbert Druks
ISBN 0-8315-0147-2
First Edition
Printed in the United States of America

Preface

The rebirth of Israel three years after the destruction of the Axis and the liberation of the concentration camps came as a tremendous shock to some of the most respected political philosophers of the world. A small population of Jews who had clung to a tenuous strand of Erez Israel, and a shattered remnant of European Jewry who had been smuggled into their ancient homeland, defied the predictions of the world. Eminent political historians such as Arnold Toynbee, who insisted the Jews were finished as a nation, were astonished. But all the Toynbees, Gobineaus and Hitlers of this earth could not refute the fact that the Jews in Israel had achieved their independence. Despite opposition from many major world powers, and the hostility of millions of Arabs, Israel was reborn.

President Harry S Truman was one of the very few world leaders who was sympathetic toward the new Jewish State. From the start of his Presidency, he sought to relieve the suffering of Europe's refugees, and he insisted that those accused of war crimes and crimes against humanity should go on trial before a world tribunal. But he was surrounded by officials like James Forrestal, Dean Acheson, George C. Marshall, Robert Lovett and Dean Rusk who did not share his sympathies. These men, and others, made persistent efforts to reverse Truman's attitude, yet the President stubbornly stood his ground. Truman supported the rebirth of Israel, and claimed it was in America's best strategic interest to do so. Truman's support, however, came only after he learned of Soviet intentions to gain a foot-hold in the Middle East.

vi   The U.S. and Israel, 1945-1973

Nor was American recognition everything. The reborn Israel was hard-pressed when its American friend agreed to uphold the U.N. arms embargo and joined with Britain in pressure tactics designed to bring Jewish withdrawal from such strategic positions as Sinai, Gaza and Jerusalem. Indeed, the friendly American President was prepared at one instance to suggest that the Israelis give up the Negev.

Some observers, such as Senator J.W. Fulbright, who once was chairman of the Senate Foreign Relations Committee, complained that Israel always received whatever it wanted from the United States. But the history of U.S. - Israeli relationships tells a far different story. Although the Israelis have had some devoted friends in America, their survival has always rested squarely on their own willpower and faith. Whatever assistance Israel may have received from the United States was provided only after the President and Congress agreed that it was in the U.S. national interest.

The survival of Israel had been uncertain ever since the day of its rebirth. In 1948-49, 1956-57, 1967 and 1973, when the survival of the Jewish State was in gravest jeopardy, American assistance was uncertain at best. In 1956, when Israel was confronted by a massive Egyptian military build-up in the Sinai and the blockade of the port of Eilat, U.S. and Soviet intervention prevented Israel from bringing the conflict to a successful end. Meanwhile, Britain and France, Israel's momentary allies, buckled under the Soviet-American pressure, and Israel was again forced to abandon an effort to secure defensible borders. While the U.S. did little to stop the Soviet invasion of Hungary during the same period, it was prepared to join U.N. sanctions and end all economic aid to Israel. The result was the spread of Soviet influence in the Middle East.

As tension between Israel and neighboring Arab states increased, the Soviet Union escalated its shipments of arms to the Middle East. In May 1967, Egypt rolled these Soviet weapons up to the Israeli border, ordered the U.N. peacekeeping forces out of the area and once again blockaded the port of Eilat. Israel soon discovered that all the promises and guarantees of the U.N. and the U.S. concerning the freedom of passage through the Straits of Tiran were worthless. The situation worsened while the community of nations stumbled ineptly through deliberations. Confronted by a situation that grew worse each hour, Israel was forced to make a preemptive strike. In six days, the Israelis destroyed the combined armies of Egypt, Syria and

Jordan while at the same time Israel gained the defensible borders that had eluded her for nearly two decades. Still there was no peace. Israel asked for direct negotiations with the Arabs, but the Arabs refused.

In October 1973, another war broke out in the Middle East. This time, Israel's political leaders waited for a political means to bring peace - and Israel was attacked. The only major power that helped Israel was the United States. President Richard M. Nixon started a massive airlift of supplies and put the entire U.S. military structure on a general alert when it appeared that the Soviet Union was preparing for intervention. But the whole tragedy of the Yom Kippur War could have been averted had Israel been supplied with sophisticated U.S. electronic surveillance equipment and critical antimissile weapons.

In 1973, as in 1956 and 1967, the Soviet Union threatened direct intervention in the Middle East. But each American President at the time of each conflict let the Soviets know that the United States considered its national security interests involved in the conflict and that intervention would not be tolerated.

Catastrophy was turned into victory in 1973. It was a miracle produced by the faith and courage of the Israeli people. It was a disaster averted by the timely arrival of American weapons and supplies.

Ever since that miraculous victory, Israel has been in political, economic and diplomatic difficulty. The ever-increasing dependency on the good will of the United States has forced Israel to make concession after concession. Israel wants peace, but it will not forfeit its chances of survival. Unlike those nations that were ready to appease and surrender to Axis demands during the 1930s and 1940s, Israel fights. It has been the spirit of constant readiness and the courage to defend itself at all costs that has prevented any power or combination of powers from forcing Israel to submit.

Israel has had to recognize that America's support is primarily based on what is best for America. For this reason, Israel must show that its friendship is of value and of benefit to America. It is not enough that the Arab states reveal their troublesome side through terrorism, oil embargos and money games. To retain, and further develop friendship with the United States, it may become necessary for Israel to develop better relations with others, including the Soviet Union. If the U.S. can seek *detente*, so can Israel.

As one studies the history of the relations between Israel and the United States, it becomes evident that the U.S. never gave the Jewish State the so-called "blank check." To date, the United States has found it to be in its best interests to provide assistance to Israel. America is a freedom-loving state, and as long as it remains so, it will probably assist states like Israel that are willing to fight for their freedom. But, as in the past, that aid will come only when the American Presidents and Congress are persuaded that the cause is worthwhile, and that the state involved is willing and able to defend itself.

Israel cannot afford another Yom Kippur War. It cannot depend on others, and it must find within its own resources a reinvigorated leadership and a greater self-reliance.

A Word of Thanks

I would like to acknowledge and thank the Manuscript division staffs of the American Jewish Committee, Brandeis University, Columbia University, the Department of State, the Library of Congress, the National Archives, the Harry S Truman Library, Yale University, and the Zionist Archives (New York) for permitting me to use the papers and records of Benjamin Akzin, the American Jewish Committee, the American Palestine Committee, the American Zionist Emergency Committee, Louis D. Brandeis, Clark Clifford, Benjamin V. Cohen, Jacob De Haas, Harry Friedenwald, Eddie Jacobson, the Jewish Agency, Juliam W. Mack, William D. Leahy, James G. McDonald, Samuel I. Rosenman, Charles Ross, Henry L. Stimson, Robert Szold, Harry S Truman, Stephen S. Wise, the World Zionist Organization, the Zionist Organization of America, and the Zionist Archives individuals files.

I am most grateful to the following individuals for granting me interviews: Benjamin Akzin, Benjamin V. Cohen, Roger P. Davies, Rabbi Israel Goldstein, Senator Charles Goodell, Raymond A. Hare, Rabbi Arthur Hertzberg, Dr. Emanuel Neumann, Richard H. Nolte, Israeli Consuls Padon and Aviloah, Samuel I. Rosenman, Ambassador Ovadiah Soffer, Robert Szold, and President Harry S Truman.

Chapter I

Truman and Israel

On April 12, 1945, Harry S Truman was sworn in as President of the United States. He had been a farmer, a soldier, a businessman, a salesman, a judge, a U.S. Senator from Missouri for a decade, and a Vice President. As Senator, he had expressed his understanding and sympathy for the plight of the Jewish people:

> It is sad to realize that the tragic world conflict still raging around the globe was started by a man whose hatred for a race became such an obsession that he refused to treat these people as human beings.
>
> Little did he reckon with the courage and endurance of a race hardened for centuries of oppression, and strengthened by a firm faith that ultimately another Moses must come to lead them out of their modern bondage and into the Promised Land.

But he also was cautious in his support of a Jewish homeland in Erez Israel as can be understood by reading his letter to the President of the Jewish National Workers' Alliance:

February 16, 1944

Mr. M. Greenwald, President
Jewish National Workers' Alliance
7460 Stanford
University City, Missouri

Dear Mr. Greenwald:

> Appreciate very much your letter of the Eighth, and I am familiar with the resolution to which you referred.
>
> It is one which affects the foreign relations program between Great Britain, the United States, and the Middle East. My sympathy of course is with the Jewish people, but I am of the opinion a resolution such as this should be very circumspectly handled until we know just exactly where we are going and why.

With the difficulty looming up between Russia and Poland, and the Balkan States and Russia, and with Great Britain and Russia absolutely necessary to us in financing the war I don't want to throw any bricks to upset the apple cart, although when the right time comes I am willing to help make the fight for a Jewish homeland in Palestine.

Sincerely yours,

(signed)

Harry S Truman

Harry Truman was a President who studied history, and he knew the history of the Jewish people. He saw historical parallels, and the plight of those who had survived the madness of the Holocaust reminded him of refugees from his own homeland who had been displaced from Missouri and Kansas by the U.S. Civil War. Truman believed that the survivors of the Nazi atrocities represented a challenge to the West and, as President, he "undertook to do something about it." Not only did he seek to punish the guilty and provide refuge for the persecuted, but he also helped to re-establish the State of Israel. No problem that he faced "was more controversial or more complex than the problem of Israel," said Truman. "And on that account," he believed, "the Jews needed some place where they could go."[1]

The man from Missouri who ended World War II, stopped Soviet expansion in Europe, the Middle East and Asia, also inaugurated a self-help concept in American foreign policy. His constant struggle for civil and human rights for all peoples had an important impact on the history of the Jews. It was Truman who insisted that there be a Nuremberg Trial to record the crimes committed by the Nazis and their collaborators. It was Harry S Truman who called on Britain to open up Palestine, and it was Harry S Truman who fought for a revision of U.S. immigration laws to permit the homeless of Europe to find a better life in America. It was Truman who invited the 982 Jews of Camp Ontario, Oswego, New York, to enter America officially and not return to Europe as Franklin D. Roosevelt had planned.

While Truman's policies toward the European refugees and Israel were motivated primarily by what was best for the United States, they reflected his strong moral affinity for the Jewish people.

After he discovered that the survivors of Hitler's concentration camps were still being kept behind the barbed wire of those camps, President Truman ordered General Eisenhower on August 31, 1945, to "get those people out of camps and into decent houses until they can be repatriated or evacuated." He also advised Eisenhower that he was "communicating directly with the British Government in an effort to have the doors of Palestine opened to such of these displaced persons as wish to go there."[2]

Truman felt keenly for the people made homeless by World War II, and he wanted to see everything possible done "at once to facilitate the entrance of some of these displaced persons and refugees into the United States." This way, America would do something to relieve the human misery and establish "an example to the other countries of the world which (were) able to receive some of these war sufferers." Very few people from Europe had managed to come to America during the war years. In 1942, only two percent of the immigration quotas had been used; in 1943, five percent; in 1944, six percent; and in 1945, seven percent. As of November 30, 1945, only ten percent of the quotas for the European countries had been used. President Truman believed "that common decency and the fundamental comradeship of all human beings" required America to reduce human suffering.[3]

Aware that Erez Israel might not be able to accommodate all the people that wanted to go there, Truman also realized that the prospect for admitting a great number of refugees to the U.S. was bleak. This was evident as he wrote to David K. Niles on April 10, 1947, "The ideal of getting 400,000 immigrants into this country, is of course, beyond our wildest dreams. If we could get 100,000 we would be doing remarkably well and I imagine there is a shortage of coatmakers."[4] On July 7, 1947, Truman asked Congress to admit the displaced persons to America. He reminded Congress that the United States was a nation founded by immigrants who had fled from oppression and that America had "thrived on the energy and diversity of many peoples." After much deliberation and debate, Congress passed the Displaced Persons Act which admitted 200,000 refugees during a two year period. Although Truman claimed the legislation discriminated "in callous fashion against displaced persons of the Jewish faith" and excluded "many persons of the Catholic faith..." he signed the measure "in order not to delay further the beginning of a resettlement program and in the expectation that the necessary remedial action will follow when the Congress reconvenes."

When the Congress did reconsider the immigration laws, five years later, it passed the Walter Immigration Act over Truman's veto. It was "incredible," Truman said, that "in this year of 1952, we should again be enacting into law such a slur on the patriotism, the capacity, and the decency of a large part of our citizenry."[5]

WAR CRIMINALS AND THEIR TRIALS

After the victory in Europe, President Truman had no doubt that the Nazis should be punished for their war crimes and their crimes against humanity. In a letter to Senator Burton K. Wheeler, dated December 21, 1945, Truman put it this way: "While we have no desire to be unduly cruel to Germany, I cannot feel any great sympathy for those who caused the death of so many human beings by starvation, disease, and outright murder...."[6] But the Allies could not agree on how to deal with the war criminals. British Foreign Minister Anthony Eden said that he wanted to see them executed on the spot. Truman insisted on court trials. And the Soviets wanted to tie the trials to well-known Nazis.[7]

An International Military Tribunal at Nuremberg, and later at Tokyo, was organized with judges from the United States, Great Britain, France and the Soviet Union. Nazi and Japanese defendants were tried for "crimes against peace," "war crimes" and "crimes against humanity." The Nuremberg, Tokyo and auxiliary tribunals brought some, but by no means all, of the war criminals to justice.

At those trials, the record was officially inscribed and the principle was established that no person could say that they could not be held accountable because they were merely following orders. Each and every defendant was held accountable for their own actions.[8]

Although the declarations of these tribunals were inspiring, their actual effectiveness was appalling. Truman had favored just prosecution of all war criminals, but by 1947, John J. McCloy, the U.S. High Commissioner for Germany, had exonerated some 200,000 young Germans from any culpability for political activities, amnestied 800,000 Germans of low economic status, and pardoned 40,000 Germans who were at least 50 percent disabled. Of the three million who could have been charged with criminal behavior as part of Hitler's Third Reich, most were never examined, only 200,000 were identified on record, and pitifully few were ever brought to a formal trial. In short, almost all the Nazis who brought death to more than a score million people in the massive executions went unpunished. Indeed, they prospered. They soon found their way back into the governments of each occupied sector of Germany where they assumed positions of authority in both civil and military administration. In Bavaria, the cradle of Nazi fascism, a full 85 percent of the Nazi-era civil servants were reinstated.

In 1948, the United Nations prepared and adopted a convention against genocide, and President Truman asked the U.S. Congress to ratify it. "We must do our part," the President said, "to outlaw forever the mass murder of innocent people."[9] But Congress failed to find wisdom in Truman's advice. To this day, the United States Congress has refused to ratify a convention against genocide.

ISRAEL

From the start of his Presidency, Truman was persistently advised by State Department officials to be cautious on the Palestine issue. They were constantly warning him that Zionist representatives were using every tactic available to obtain commitments for unlimited immigration to the British mandate in the Middle East.

Secretary of State Edward Stettinius cautioned Truman of "Zionist leaders who sought to press for unlimited Jewish immigration into Palestine and the establishment of a Jewish state." Stettinius urged Truman to exercise "the greatest care" and to keep "the long-range interests of the country" in mind.[10] Acting Secretary of State Joseph C. Grew also wrote to Truman, and said that all he really need do was to assure the Zionists that their views would be given careful consideration.[11]

David Ben Gurion contacted the State Department clique and informed them that the Jews were tired of waiting. Allied leaders had placated the Jews, Ben Gurion said, and made them "believe that they would eventually see the fruition of their aims in Palestine if only they kept quiet during the European war." The war was over, the Zionist statesman informed them, and the Jews could no longer wait. Jews will "fight if necessary, in defense of their rights and the consequences would be on Great Britain's head...."[12]

Truman was skeptical of the views and attitudes expressed by the "striped pants boys" of the State Department who were so coldly indifferent to the Jews. He felt that America's long range goals for world peace would "be best served by a solution that would accord justice to the needs and the wants of the Jewish people who had so long been persecuted."[13] And he found the American people firmly in favor of establishing a Jewish homeland in Palestine. On July 3, 1945, Senator Robert F. Wagner sent Truman a letter signed by 54 Senators and 250 Representatives requesting him to pressure the British to open up Palestine.

Truman reassured the Arab states, however, that the United States would take no action regarding "the basic situation in Palestine" without consulting both them and the Jews. Meanwhile, he sent Dean Earl G. Harrison, of the University of Pennsylvania Law School, to investigate conditions for the displaced persons. Harrison's findings were heartbreaking. The refugees were still in concentration camps and they had little hope for the future. Few wanted to return to their old homes, and Harrison recommended that they be admitted to Erez Israel. He reported that anyone visiting the concentration camps would find it "nothing short of calamitous to contemplate that the gates of Palestine should be soon closed."[14]

Truman wanted to examine the Palestine question at the Potsdam Conference and, on July 24, wrote British Prime Minister Winston Churchill that Americans were "fervently" urging that the 1939 White Paper restricting Jewish immigration to Palestine be lifted. Truman added that he hoped Churchill would "without delay...lift the restrictions...." Perhaps, Truman said, there won't be time to consider the Palestine question in depth at Potsdam, but greater delay would only compound the difficulties. He asked for Churchill's views so that they could "at a later, but not too distant date, discuss the problem in concrete terms."[15]

During the Potsdam Conference of late July and early August 1945, which was called to resolve Allied differences over the future peace and to insure Soviet entry into the Pacific war, Truman asked Churchill to support the establishment of a Jewish homeland in Palestine. But the British leader prefered to see the Jewish homeland established elsewhere - possibly Tripoli.

After Potsdam, reporters asked if any progress had been made on the Palestine matter and Truman replied it had been discussed with Churchill and Attlee, and that it was still being discussed. When they asked him if he had taken the issue up with Stalin, Truman replied that there was nothing Stalin could do about it. Truman said that he wanted to see as many Jews as possible enter Palestine, and he believed it could be worked out diplomatically with the British and the Arabs.[16]

On August 31, 1945, Truman urged Clement Attlee, Britain's newly elected Prime Minister, to permit 100,000 Jews confined in European displaced persons (DP) camps to enter Palestine. While the Nazi extermination programs had killed many of the pre-war Jews who had wished to emigrate, Truman said, there were still many who want to do so and the American people firmly believe that Britain should not bar a reasonable number of these survivors from settling in their ancient homeland. No claim was "more meritorious than that of groups who for so many years have known persecution and enslavement."[17]

Such remarks upset the Arabs. The Iraqis, for example, issued a warning that it would be unwise for the United States to fall from favor with the 40 million Arabs in the Middle East.[18]

THE ANGLO-AMERICAN COMMITTEE OF INQUIRY

The British balked at Truman's suggestion of admitting 100,000 Jews into Palestine. Instead, they called for the creation of an inquiry commission. Truman reacted by insisting that if there was to be a commission, its focus must be on Palestine. Moreover, he demanded speedy action. He got his way.

When the American members of the Anglo-American Committee ran into obstinate opposition from their British counterparts, David Niles suggested that Truman send the following message to the American delegation:

> The world expectantly awaits a report from the entire Commission which will be the basis of an affirmative program to relieve untold suffering and misery. In the deliberations now going on, and in the report which will evolve from them, it is my deep and sincere wish that the American delegation shall stand firm for a program that is in accord with the highest American tradition of generosity and justice.

On April 18, Truman sent Niles a brief letter: "Thanks for...the suggested message. It was sent."[19]

The Anglo-American Committee concluded that the 100,000 Jews should be admitted to Palestine immediately. But the British, after having promised to accept any decision reached by the Anglo-American Committee, rejected its findings. British Foreign Minister Ernest Bevin urged a delay in the publication of the commission's report. He complained that the Jews were bringing people capable of bearing arms into Palestine, and that because of their "aggressive attitude, were poisoning relations between our two peoples." The British insisted that Jews in Palestine disarm themselves and that the United States start preparing for military, as well as economic assistance to the area because His Majesty's Government was considering complete withdrawal from Palestine.[20]

Truman welcomed the committee's report.[21] And he was especially pleased that the document recommended "the abrogation of the White Paper of 1939...."[22]

The U.S. Joint Chiefs of Staff advised the President to stay out of the Middle East, warning that if America entered the area it would alienate the Arabs and foster Soviet penetration there.[23] But many other Americans, like Congressman Herman P. Eberhalter of Pennsylvania, felt that there had been enough procrastination. He believed it was time for action, saying "One cannot fail to have some suspicion that delay is being purposely used with the hope that perhaps some other 'solution' than the actual transference may be accomplished."[24] The President agreed.

When the British called for further discussion of "43 subjects" concerning Palestine, Truman replied that the 100,000 Jews must first be admitted to Erez Israel, and then the experts could be brought in to split hairs.[25] Moreover, Truman said he was prepared to tackle the physical problems and provide all the ships necessary to transport the Jews to Palestine.

On June 11, Truman announced the establishment of a Cabinet Committee on Palestine that would help determine and implement the U.S. Government's policies on Palestine. Bevin replied harshly with a public statement that accused Truman of wanting to push Jews into Palestine because he did not want them in the United States.

A week later, on June 18, the Haganah, the Jewish defense force in Erez Israel, blew up eight bridges along their frontiers. Within another week, Prime Minister Attlee retaliated with repressive measures against the Yishuv. Jerusalem was placed under curfew and more than 2,600 people were arrested.

Under these circumstances, Truman met with American members of the Jewish Agency and told them he was determined to see the transfer of "100,000 Jewish immigrants to Palestine with all dispatch." The President also promised "technical and financial" support for the "transportation of the immigrants from Europe to Palestine."

The Jewish Agency delegates were back to Truman within a week, writing him about their concern over reports that the British were insisting on an "exhaustive diplomatic schedule" before any action would be taken on the admittance of the 100,000. They found "the statements emanating from London inimical or hostile to the whole spirit of the constructive proposals contained in the report of the Anglo-American Committee."

Cabinet committees met to discuss the Anglo-American Committee's recommendations, but since Truman refused to assume military responsibility for Palestine, he had little bargaining power. The Morrison-Grady Plan, which the committees eventually devised, was no more than another British "White Paper" that called for a strong central government to rule over two apparently autonomous states. Only 1,500 out of the area's 45,000 square miles was to come under Jewish control; the central government was to retain control over Jerusalem, Bethlehem and the Negev; and Arab approval would be necessary before the 100,000 Jews could be landed on the Levantine shore.

Concerned by the Morrison-Grady Plan, American Zionists approached James G. McDonald and asked him to see Truman on their behalf. McDonald agreed and met with the President on July 27, 1946. The session was stormy for Truman had become angry and unhappy because of the Palestine pressures. He complained to McDonald that the Zionists didn't understand the significance of the plan and were acting foolishly. But McDonald insisted that the implications of the plan were well understood and that the Jews would rather not have the 100,000 refugees admitted if it meant the acceptance of a terrible plan.

He told him that if he got the 100,000 at this price, he would "go down in history as anathema." Truman "exploded" at the remark, but couldn't intimidate McDonald who shot back that even "if indirectly he gave assent to this thing, he would be responsible for scrapping the Jewish interests in Palestine."

"Well," said Truman, "you can't satisfy these people." He said that he'd strive to get the 100,000 into Palestine, but the "Jews aren't going to write the history of the United States or my history."

President Roosevelt had understood "some of the imponder-
ables," McDonald pointed out.

"But I am not Roosevelt," Truman shot back. "I am not from
New York. I am from the Middle West."

"I have no object in coming to see you except to tell the truth,"
McDonald pleaded.

"I want to hear it," Truman replied. "I hear it too seldom."

"Well," continued McDonald, "the moderation of the Jewish
leaders is shown by the fact that they have asked me to see you."

"They knew I wouldn't receive some of them," answered Truman.

McDonald found Truman "hell-bent on the 100,000," but he
would not "assume any more responsibility than the $45 million
obligation." Truman told McDonald that he didn't care about partition of Palestine. "It is not my business. You can't satisfy the Jews
anyway. You have got to get the British to agree."[26]

"Well, Mr. President," McDonald said, "you can make them
agree at too high a price."

"We got them to agree," Truman said.

"Yes, but it was too high a price. I think you can get the British to
agree if you will be firm and insist on it and refuse to have anything to
do with these other matters."

McDonald tried to follow a prepared memorandum, but Truman
often interrupted him to complain about how ungrateful everybody
was, and how badly served he was: "I can't get the right people."[27]

By August 12, Truman decided to reject the plan, and he wrote
Attlee to that effect.

But Truman still couldn't find his way clear of the Palestine issue.
Britain had ignored the Anglo-American recommendations and his
own requests that 100,000 Jews be admitted. Moreover, the Cabinet
committees had failed and the Republican Party leader, Thomas
Dewey of New York, issued strong statements in favor of Jewish
immigration to Palestine.

On October 3, Truman advised Attlee that he would soon issue a
statement in favor of Jewish immigration to Palestine. A day later,
on Yom Kippur, he made a public address that called on the British to
admit 100,000 Jews to their ancient homeland.

Soon thereafter, Truman wrote to Senator Walter F. George saying that he wished all members of Congress could visit the Displaced

Persons camps of Europe to see precisely what was happening to a half-million human beings "through no fault of their own." Every effort had to be made to get "these people properly located...." he said. As far as he was concerned, there was no reason "in the world why 100,000 Jews could not go to Palestine," nor was there any reason why America could not allow the unused northern European immigration quotas to be used by refugees.[28]

Attlee was sulking in a huff and progress on the Palestine issue was stalled; Truman decided to move. On October 10, 1946, he wrote the British Prime Minister saying that if his October 4 statement had been embarassing, he regretted it, but he "could not even for a single day postpone" making clear America's interest in seeing substantial Jewish immigration to Palestine. The Jews had suffered tremendously, he wrote, and the world should not make them suffer further by keeping them suspended and wondering about what the morrow will bring. Further postponement would make the solution to Palestine even more difficult.[29]

The British and the Arabs didn't like Truman's position, and they let him know it. Ibn Saud wrote Truman on October 15, 1946, saying that the Jews were aggressors and he was astonished by the President's statements.[30] Truman replied to Saud by saying that all parties concerned had "a common responsibility for working out a solution" to permit those who must leave Europe to find a home where they could "dwell in peace and security." America supported the entry of Jews into Palestine, he said, advising Saud that, as President, he would still seek to consult with both Arabs and Jews.[31]

The British had tried to sponsor Jewish-Arab negotiations in London, but when these talks proved fruitless, the whole issue was submitted to the United Nations on February 18, 1947.

Foreign Secretary Bevin accused Truman of using the Palestine question to gain votes in the 1946 elections, and the White House replied that America's interest in Palestine was "of long and continuing standing." It was "a deep and abiding interest shared by our people without regard to their political affiliation."

Many Americans and their representatives were greatly disturbed by the stubborn and unfriendly British attitude and suggested that America should not help Britain in Greece and Turkey unless the British became more cooperative in Palestine. Representative Chet Holifeld, during the Congressional debate on aide to Greece and

Turkey[32], suggested that America strike a bargain. "We support Britain if Britain admits the 100,000 Jews to Palestine."[33] Some tried to persuade Congress to defeat the loan to Britain, or at least to delay it a few months. They hoped that this might show the British that they could not do whatever pleased them.[34]

While Congressman Holifeld's suggestions might have been interesting, they were hardly feasible. The United States was trying to help Greece and Turkey remain free of Soviet control. The Truman Doctrine was not directed just toward helping the British, but toward all free nations.

Great Britain's request for U.N. General Assembly action was formally received on April 2, 1947, and on May 15, the United Nations created a special committee called UNSCOP to study the Palestine question. UNSCOP was composed of representatives from Australia, Canada, Czechoslovakia, Guatemala, India, Iran, Netherlands, Peru, Sweden, Uruguay and Yugoslavia. All governments and peoples were asked to refrain from using force or any other action which might prejudice a settlement.

Secretary of State George C. Marshall advised Truman to issue a statement asking Americans to abide by the U.N. request. Even though such a statement might irritate certain groups who actively supported illegal immigration to Palestine, he felt it should be issued to put the world on notice that the U.S. did not support "activities of American citizens or residents of a character which might render more difficult the task which the U.N. has assumed."[35] Truman agreed and issued the statement on June 5, 1947.

THE EXODUS

The story of the *Exodus 1947* began in 1934 when the first immigrant ships secretly landed in Palestine in defiance of British restrictions. In that year, some 42,000 Jews immigrated to Erez Israel.[36] A number of Zionist spokesmen, like R. Lichtheim of Switzerland, might have been willing to discourage Jewish immigration during this most critical period, but the Jews of Palestine continued to work to save their brethern.[37]

Palestinian Jewry did not heed some Jewish Agency officials and others who advised curtailment of immigration. In early 1938, a new immigration campaign was started.

Help and money was needed, yet the rich and influential Jewish organizations of Europe and America remained, for the most part, indifferent and inept. But when the British issued their White Paper in May, 1939, Jewish leadership, from the very moderates like Weizmann to leaders of the radical Irgun, called for increased illegal immigration and total disregard of artificial quotas and restrictions set by the British.[38]

The unity of sentiment came too late. Within months, the Second World War sealed the fate of European Jewry and six million died because they were prevented from returning to Erez Israel.

By early July 1947, there were about 400,000 Jewish survivors of the Holocaust who wanted to leave Europe. They wanted to return to the place that each Passover they prayed for: "Next year in Jerusalem!" Between May and December 1945, 4,400 Jews were smuggled into Palestine. In January 1946, one ship brought 900 more. In March, two ships came with 2,000 and in May, another 3,000 arrived. By December 1946, 23,000 Jewish survivors of the war had entered Palestine illegally. They broke through British lines. Some swam ashore under cover of darkness. Many were captured and sent to British internment camps on Cyprus.

And then there was the *Exodus*.

The Jewish underground purchased an old 4,000 ton Mississippi River steamer known as *The President Warfield* and piloted it into the small Riviera port of Sete in July 1947. The ship took on more than 4,500 Jewish refugees whose one hope was to go to Erez Israel.

Five minutes before the ship was to cast off on its journey to the Levantine coast, the British intervened. A British official warned France that if the ship was permitted to leave port, Anglo-French relationships would be irreparably damaged. Paris sent an eight-word message to Sete: "Halt, the ship is not permitted to sail." The Jews tried to bribe a French port pilot with a million francs, but the British blocked the deal. The Jews then defied the British and cast off the mooring lines and set sail without a pilot.[39]

Despite many hazards, the ship made it out to sea where it was confronted by British destroyers in international waters 22 miles off the coast of Israel. The name *The President Warfield* had been covered and a new name was painted on the vessel: *Exodus 1947*. And the blue and white Jewish flag was raised, just in case the British mistook the ship's identity.

The sparkling white British destroyers were at general quarters and ordered *Exodus* to stop engines and prepare for towing. The Jews replied:

> On the deck of this boat, the *Exodus*, are 4,500 people, men, women and children, whose only crime is that they were born Jews. We are going to our country by right and not by permission of anyone....we shall never recognize a law forbidding Jews to enter their country.

[handwritten marginalia: by what right? who gave you the right]

The British flotilla drew up along side the *Exodus* and, without warning, opened fire with machine guns aimed at her bridge. Two destroyers rammed against the wooden sides of the refugee ship, and sent a boarding party of sailors and Royal Marines aboard to take control of the wheelhouse. In the battle, Bill Bernstein, an American sailor, was killed.

The refugees and the Haganah counter-attacked, retook the wheelhouse and captured the boarding party. Three British sailors were taken captive and the rest were thrown overboard. *Exodus* continued toward shore.

The British destroyers resumed ramming *Exodus* and sent another boarding party aboard. This time they bombarded the immigrant ship with gas bombs that sent dozens of refugees spralling across the deck. Two were killed. But there was another counter-attack, and this time, thirty British sailors were captured by the Jews. All through the fight, *Exodus'* radio kept transmitting a running account to receivers in Palestine.

Three hours after the first encounter, water started to flood into the battered *Exodus*. With his ship starting to sink and his decks cluttered with exhausted, wounded and dead refugees, *Exodus'* commander had no alternative and surrendered to the British warships. *Exodus* was towed to Haifa where the refugees were immediately transferred to three deportation ships which were soon steaming back across the Mediterranean. Once at sea, the British informed the refugees that they were not going to the British camps on Cyprus. They were going back to Europe.

The British wanted to teach the Jews a lesson. But what had the Jews done to deserve the harsh treatment? They had survived the Nazi Holocaust. They had dared to return to their homeland and escape the brutality of Western civilization. Was that Foreign Minister Bevin's reason for wanting to teach the Jews a lesson?

Jews in Palestine reacted with unusual violence to the fate of *Exodus*. British military installations were attacked, oil pipelines were sabotaged and British troops shot. A radar station on Mount Carmel was destroyed, and a British transport sunk. But nothing could help the 4,500 of the *Exodus*. When the refugees reached Europe, no nation would admit them, so the British shipped them back to camps in Germany.

After weeks aboard ship, many of the refugees were too weak to resist, but those with strength did fight. *Exodus* left an impact on the world, and on the members of UNSCOP who watched while the British transferred Jews to the prison ships. They never forgot the "very tired and poor,"[41] who were manhandled by the British Army.

UNSCOP REPORT

American diplomats were generally opposed to the partition of Palestine as they envisioned a truncated Jewish State without Jerusalem and without the Negev. The U.N. Special Commission on Palestine, however, did not share the State Department's view. After an extensive investigation, the United Nations unit recommended a termination of the British mandate in Palestine and the creation, without delay, and under U.N. auspices, of two states. The two states, one Jewish and the other Arab, were to be tied by an economic union. The Negev was to be in the Jewish sector and Jerusalem was to be placed under U.N. trusteeship.

Some Jews had mixed feelings about this proposal since they considered all of Palestine to be their homeland. But others saw the partition plan as an opportunity to realize the dream of a Jewish State. The Arabs were absolutely opposed to partition, and they prepared for war.

President Truman was much more partial to the creation of a Jewish State than were the British who incidentally had drafted the Balfour Declaration which viewed "with favour" the creation of a Jewish Homeland in Palestine thirty years before. But Truman wanted peace in the world and he wanted to see promises kept.

Meanwhile, the U.S. State Department continued to work against Truman and used every conceivable trick to prevent the partition and the rebirth of the Jewish State. While UNSCOP's majority report recommended the partition with the Negev and the port of Eilat going to the Jewish State, some State Department officials allied themselves with Arab and British interests in opposition to the creation of a viable Israel. The U.S. delegation to the U.N. was adamantly opposed to the boundaries recommended by UNSCOP.

According to Eliahu Elath, who was Director of the Jewish Agency's political office in Washington and a member of the Jewish Agency delegation to the U.N. General Assembly, the British wanted to maintain control of the route through the Negev and the Gulf of Eilat to Sinai. American military and political officials were also very much concerned with Soviet expansion in the Middle East and they tended to support strong British bases there rather than extend U.S. military commitments.[42] Thus, the U.S. delegation to the U.N. was instructed to help improve Galilee boundaries in favor of the Jews in return for a concession in the Negev.[43]

The Jewish Agency refused to yield the Negev and, as the United States was not prepared to support the UNSCOP recommendation on boundaries, it appeared that the two-thirds vote necessary for the General Assembly to adopt partition would not be secured. Prospects for the future Jewish State were dim and on November 17, 1947, a delegation representing the future Jewish State asked Dr. Chaim Weizmann to call on President Truman as soon as possible to secure his help. A call was made to the White House and, within an hour, Dr. Weizmann was informed that President Truman would be pleased to see him on November 19.[44]

Supreme Court Justice Felix Frankfurter met Dr. Weizmann and his party at Washington's Union Station and accompanied the group to the Shoreham Hotel. The next day, Eliahu Epstein (Elath) gave Weizmann the *aide-memoire* on the port of Eilat, a document which set the port in a geographical perspective of being Israel's only sea access to Asia, East Africa and Australia. A map of the Negev, with a plan for future development, was appended to the *aide-memoire* which Weizmann took with him when he went to see Truman.

Dr. Weizmann was advised to take up only one issue with Truman: the fate of Eilat. It was felt that there wouldn't be time for serious discussion of several issues and, if he presented the President with only one matter, and there was time to explain it fully, there would be a better chance for success because Truman might not want to see Weizmann leave empty-handed.[45]

When they entered the White House at noon, Weizmann was invited to proceed directly to the President's office while Elath and the rest of the party remained in outside offices with Clifford and Niles.

Weizmann spoke with Truman for half an hour and, when he came out of the session, "his face showed signs of great satisfaction."[46] Weizmann had told Truman of the importance of the Negev to the future Jewish State. He spoke of the agricultural plantations, of carrots, potatoes and bananas that had been developed with success in the arid desert. Truman, having been a farmer himself, was fascinated by the agronomy involved and sympathized with the agricultural plans. Weizmann then produced a map of the future Israel with a circle drawn about the Gulf of Eilat. Explaining that the waterway was then of little use to anybody, Weizmann showed Truman how the Jews planned to expand the area and make it an important trade route.

President Truman found the Negev-Eilat question interesting "in its widest aspects,"[47] and promised to do all he could to provide a constructive solution. Weizmann asked for U.S. support on the boundary questions and the President agreed to provide it. He also informed Weizmann that he would personally give clear instructions to his delegation at the U.N. about the Negev and Eilat.[48]

But while Truman was assuring Weizmann, the State Department was instructing Herschel Johnson, Chief of the U.S. Delegation to the United Nations, that he should inform the Jews that the United States would not be supporting the inclusion of Eilat within the borders of the future Jewish State and that the Negev would become part of the future Arab State.

At 3 p.m., Johnson saw Moshe Shertok of the Jewish Delegation in the lobby of U.N. headquarters at Lake Success. Johnson approached Shertok and was about to deliver the bad news when he was interrupted by an aide. Johnson didn't want to be bothered. But the aide persisted: "The President is on the line." Johnson went to the telephone and returned a few minutes later, apologizing to Shertok for making him wait for a conversation which, he said, "could be continued on another occassion."

PARTITION VOTE

The vote for the partition of Palestine into Jewish and Arab states came before the U.N. General Assembly on November 29, 1947. Thirty-three member states voted in favor of the partition, thirteen were opposed, and ten, including Great Britain, abstained. The State of Israel was to be born under the aegis of the community of nations. The U.N. Security Council was then instructed to develop a plan of partition, but received no instructions on how to do it.

As the Assembly voted for the partition, the Arab delegates denounced the resolution and declared their determination to block the plan. While the U.N. deliberated, Palestinian and other Arabs openly recruited by the neighboring governments of Syria, Egypt, Jordan and Iraq, planned to exterminate the Jews of Palestine. On November 30, eight Jews were killed. An Arab general strike was called in Palestine and violence erupted in nearly all its cities. On January 9, 1948, an armed invasion was launched by the Syrian-based "Arab Army of Liberation." Within a week, hundreds of Jews and Arabs were killed and wounded. On January 15, the Jewish Agency advised the United Nations that an international peace keeping force was needed in Palestine, but Secretary General Trygve Lie was unable to find volunteers.

The British mandate was scheduled to expire as of May 15, 1948, but President Truman had reports delivered to him on February 13, that the Arabs would begin full-scale military operations against the Jews in March. Truman appealed for peace and tried to bring an end to the fighting in Palestine through the Security Council, but with little success.

The Jews needed weapons. Without them, they faced certain extermination, and Ben Gurion sent emissaries around Europe to purchase rifles, machine guns, aircraft, artillery and tanks.

Meanwhile, the British worked relentlessly to prevent able-bodied Jewish refugees from entering Palestine while they threw ever-increasing support to the Arabs. The Jews turned to America, hoping that the U.S. might sell weapons, but that hope was shattered by the strict U.S. embargo on all weapons destined for the Middle East. In the end, it was the Soviet Union that encouraged Czechoslovakia to sell arms to the Jews. The Soviets hoped to see an end to the British imperialist influence in the Mediterranean.[49]

Pressures on Truman increased. Pro-Arab and pro-Israeli spokesmen courted his favor. But the President refused to see any of them.

Eddie Jacobson, Truman's friend and former business partner from Missouri, however, could get into the White House. On February 21, Jacobson wrote Truman: "...I have asked you very little in the way of favors during all our years of friendship, but am begging of you to see Dr. Weizmann as soon as possible."[50] A few days later, Truman replied there wasn't anything that anyone could say on the Palestine question that he had not already heard. Jacobson went to Washington anyway, and years later he recalled what happened when he got there.

I came to the White House on Saturday, March 13, and was greeted by Matt Connelly who advised...and begged me not discuss Palestine with the President. I quickly told Matt that that's what I came to Washington for and I was determined to discuss this very subject with the President. When I entered the President's office, I noticed with pleasure that he looked well, that his trip to Florida did him good. For a few minutes we discussed our families...and other personal things.

I then brought up the Palestine subject. He was abrupt in speech and very bitter in the words he was throwing my way. In all the years of our friendship he never talked to me in this manner....

Truman made it difficult for Jacobson to continue, but his old friend argued back from every possible angle. He reminded him of his feelings for Dr. Weizmann, which Truman had often expressed to Jacobson. He told him that Dr. Weizmann was a sick man, and that nevertheless, he had made this long journey to the United States especially to see the President. Truman would not be moved. Jacobson then glanced at a striking statue of Andrew Jackson that was in the room and was inspired to say:

Harry, all your life you have had a hero. You are probably the best read man on the life of Andrew Jackson. I remember when we had our store together and you were always reading books and papers and pamphlets on this great American. Well, Harry, I too have a hero....I, too, studied his past and I agree with you as you have often told me, that he is a gentleman and a great statesman as well. I am talking about Chaim Weizmann ....Now you refuse to see him because you were insulted by some of our American Jewish leaders...It doesn't sound like you, Harry, because I thought that you could take this stuff they have been handing out to you.[51]

Jacobson had finished. Truman began to drum his fingers on his desk, stared out the window into the rose garden, just over his family pictures and then passed a few seconds in silence. For Jacobson, those seconds seemed eternal. And then the President looked his old friend square in the eyes and said: "You win, you baldheaded SOB, I will see him."[52]

---

1 Harry S Truman, *Decision: At War with the Experts,* Television production by Screen Gems, Inc.

2 Judah Nadich, *Eisenhower and the Jews* (New York, 1953), 113-114.

3 *Public Papers of Harry S Truman,* December 22, 1945.

4 Harry S Truman to David K. Niles, Harry S Truman Library. According to Saul S. Friedman's *No Haven for the Oppressed* (Detroit, 1973), the Stratton Displaced Persons Bill of 1947 resulted in the admission of only 2,499 Jews out of a total of 220,000 persons admitted.

5 *Public Papers of Harry S Truman,* June 25, 1950.

6 Samuel I. Rosenman Papers, Harry S Truman Library.

7 U.S. Department of State, The Conference of Berlin (The Potsdam Conference) (Two vols., Washington, 1960) July 31, 1945, 537-539. Hereafter cited as *Potsdam Conference.*

8 Interview with Samuel I. Rosenman, April 19, 1961.

9 *Public Papers of Harry S Truman,* June 27, 1950.

10 Harry S Truman, *Years of Trial and Hope,* (New York, 1956), 69. Hereafter cited as *Years of Trial and Hope.*

11 *Ibid.,* 134.

12 *Foreign Relations of the United States,* June 27, 1945, VIII, 713-715.

13 *Years of Trial and Hope,* 134-135.

14 *Ibid.,* 137.

15 *Ibid.,* 135-136.

16 *Potsdam Conference,* II, 1407; *Foreign Relations Papers,* August 18, 1945, VIII, 722; *Public Papers of Harry S Truman,* 228.

17 Harry S Truman to Prime Minister Attlee, August 31, 1945, President's Official File 204, Harry S Truman Libarary.

18 *Foreign Relations Papers,* August 20, 1945, VIII, 723-724.

19 Papers of Harry S Truman, Official File, Harry S Truman Library.

20 *Foreign Relations Papers,* April 27, 1946, VIII, 587-588.

21 *Public Papers of Harry S Truman,* April 30, 1946.

22 *Foreign Relations Papers,* May 1, 1946, VIII, 589-590.

23 Papers of Harry S Truman, Official File, Harry S Truman Library.

24 Herman P. Eberhalter to President Harry S Truman, May 23, 1946, President's Official File 204, Harry S Truman Library.

25 Truman, *Years of Trial and Hope,* 148-149; *The New York Times,* May 5, 1946; *Foreign Relations Papers,* June 21, 1946, 632-633.

26 James G. McDonald interview with President Truman, July 27, 1946, Benjamin Akzin File, The Zionist Emergency Council Papers, Zionist Archives, New York.

27 *Ibid.*

28 While the U.S. may have been more inclined to support the creation of a Jewish homeland than Great Britain, some wondered about U.S. policies. Bartley Crum, a member of the Anglo-American Commission charged that the State Department was infested with anti-Semites. And former Secretary of the Interior Harold Ickes wondered why the Balfour Declaration had not been implemented almost two years after World War II. "What price Jewish blood in terms of Saudi Arabian oil?" See *New York Herald Tribune,* August 22, 1946, and *The New York Times,* December 9, 1946.

President Truman to Walter F. George, October 8, 1946, Stephen S. Wise

Papers, Brandeis University.

29 President Truman to Clement Attlee, October 10, 1946, Harry S Truman Library.

30 King Saud to President Truman, October 15, 1946, Official File 204, Harry S Truman Library; *The New York Times,* October 18, 29, 1946.

31 President Truman to King Saud, October 25, 1946, Official File 204, Harry S Truman Library; *Foreign Relations Papers,* October 25, 1946, 714-717.

32 On February 26, the British Ambassador to Washington called on Secretary of State Marshall with an urgent request from Bevin for aid. The British said that they would have to withdraw their support from Greece and Turkey.

33 *Congressional Record,* April 1, 1947, 2995-2996; *The New York Times,* April 1, 1947.

34 Interview with Dr. Emanuel Neumann, May 6, 1971.

35 General Marshall to President Truman, Presidents Official File 204, undated, Harry S Truman Library.

36 Chaim Weizmann to Justice Felix Frankfurter, Henry Morgenthau and Rabbi Stephen S. Wise, May 1, 1947, Stephen S. Wise Papers, Brandeis University. Jon and David Kimche, *The Secret Roads* (London, 1954), 30. Hereafter cited as Kimche, *Secret Roads.*

37 *Ibid.*

38 Emanuel Neumann, *In the Arena, An Autobiographical Memoir* (New York, 1976) 142-148. Hereafter cited as *In the Arena.* R. Lichtheim to N. Goldmann, September 9, 1942, Jewish Agency Papers, Zionist Archives, New York.

39 David C. Holly, *Exodus 1947,* (Boston 1969).

40 Robert St. John, *Eban* (New York, 1972) 168-169.

41 *Ibid.*

42 Eliahu Elath, *Israel and Elath: The Political Struggle for the Inclusion of Elath in the Jewish State,* (London, 1966), 10. Hereafter cited as Elath, *Israel and Elath.*

43 *Ibid.,* 13.

44 *Ibid.*

45 *Ibid.*

46 *Ibid.,* 19-20.

47 *Ibid.,* 22-23.

48 *Ibid.*

49 Kimche, *Secret Roads,* 70.

50 Eddie Jacobson to Matt Connelly, Eddie Jacobson Papers, Zionist Archives, New York.

51 From Harry S Truman Library, and Zionist Archives, New York.

52 *Ibid.*

Chapter II

From Trusteeship to Recognition

The day after Weizmann saw Truman, Ambassador Warren Austin announced a reversal in the U.S. position. Austin declared that the General Assembly vote of November 29, 1947, was merely a "recommendation" and not a binding decision. Since peace was at stake, he proposed the establishment of a U.N. trusteeship for Palestine in which Great Britain would continue to hold the Palestine Mandate. Austin's speech apparently was a rude awakening for many, including President Truman.[1]

Some officials of the State and Defense departments had honest differences of opinion with the President, but as Truman noted in his calendar, there were individuals who always wanted to cut his throat, and with this act, they had succeeded.[2] Still others were simply bigots. "I am sorry to say," Truman wrote in his memoirs, "there were some among them who were also inclined to be anti-Semitic."[3]

After the Partition vote, those State Department officials who had opposed Truman predicted that the United States would lose bases, oil concessions, trade and religious institutions, and that there would be a setback in the European Recovery Plan because of the loss of oil. Moreover, Cold War warriors like George F. Kennan and James Forrestal argued that the Soviet Union would increase its influence in the Middle East and Europe because of U.S. support for the Jewish State.[4] Dean Rusk, who led the State Department's U.N. division, called for a reversal of the Partition vote.[5]

At a National Security Council session on February 17, 1948, General Alfred Gruenther estimated that between 80,000 and 160,

000 U.S. troops would be required to enforce the partition of Palestine.[6] The NSC also considered a State Department draft report that said any solution to the Palestine problem that brought the Soviet Union into the area, or resulted in continued hostility, would be a danger to U.S. security. Some military people wanted to scrap the Partition idea and generally agreed with State Department officials who wanted to diplomatically reconsider the Partition vote and then maneuver into a position of endorsing continued British trusteeship of the area.

Meanwhile, the Central Intelligence Agency presented the NSC with a false report that said the British had been impartial in their attempts to curb Arab-Jewish hostilities.[7] Then, backed by the CIA, the National Security Council adopted Dean Rusk's proposal for the creation of a trusteeship that would receive U.S. military support so it would be able to "maintain internal order."

President Truman had been given a proposed draft of a U.N. speech that mentioned trusteeship as a temporary solution. He glanced at it and remarked that it looked all right, but that he had not made a formal approval of a "final draft on the question."[8] Furthermore, he had tried to make it clear to Secretary Marshall that "nothing should be presented to the Security Council that could be interpreted as a recession on our part from the position we took in the General Assembly." He ordered Marshall to send him the "final draft of Austin's remarks....for his consideration."[9] This was not done.

White House advisor Clark Clifford became alarmed by the anti-partition sentiment among Senate, Defense and CIA officialdom. In early March, he submitted a memo presenting arguments in favor of Partition to Truman. Delay, Clifford warned, could only result in a more unstable world situation and, unless the U.N. implemented Partition, the Soviets might intervene on the pretense of preserving world peace and defending the U.N. Charter.

Soviet minister Andrei Gromyko, on December 30, 1947, had already called for measures to insure the "speediest and most effective implementation of Partition."

There were some who claimed that the Arabs would not sell their oil if the United States supported the U.N. Partition plan, but the Arabs needed the U.S. more than the U.S. needed them. With or without Partition, the Arabs would continue selling oil to the West.

They "must have oil royalties or go broke." The Arab "social and economic structure would be irreparably harmed by adopting a Soviet orientation...." and the Arabs would be "committing suicide." Moreover, World War II had taught us strategic supplies such as oil should be made available closer to home. It was time to develop resources in Colorado, Utah and Wyoming. Clifford's memo also claimed that a failure to implement the U.N.'s Partition decision because of U.S. diplomacy would damage both U.N. and U.S. reputations. America's world image was already damaged, Clifford said, and he could not see how the Soviet Union, or any other nation, could treat the U.S. with anything but contempt because of its "shilly-shalling appeasement of the Arabs."

We would give the appearance of having "no foreign policy," of not knowing "where we are going," of Presidential bewilderment, of "trembling before threats of a few nomadic desert tribes." The Arabs themselves would have greater respect for the United States if we appeased them less, Clifford argued, and Arab opposition to Partition was not so much a defiance of the U.N. Partition vote as it was a "deliberate and insolent defiance of the Untied States."

Furthermore, he said, Britain was economically exhausted and, to make up for her inability to keep an adequate military force, she turned to making alliances with Moslems from Pakistan to North Africa, but those alliances were not nearly as important to the United States.

Finally, Clifford argued that according to "competent military authorities," the Jews of Palestine were well trained and capable of coping with "any forces the Arabs could throw against them," provided they could get equipment. The Jews were strongly pro-American while the Arabs were not. And the Jews would keep that position unless the Soviets undertook unilateral intervention.[10]

Clifford concluded his memo by proposing that the United States call on the U.N. Security Council to invoke economic and diplomatic sanctions against Arab states because of their acts of aggression, that the U.S. embargo on arms to the Middle East be lifted, that Britain be compelled to cooperate with the implementation of Partition, and that an international security force be established to enforce the Partition. He was sure that, under any circumstances, President Truman would do what was "best for America," even if it meant "the defeat of the Democratic Party."[11]

Truman discovered Austin's speech by reading the morning newspapers and called Clifford in for an explanation. The President was shocked and couldn't understand how Austin could have made a speech that arbitrarily reversed U.S. policy. Furthermore, he was upset because it defied everything he had told Weizmann. "Isn't that hell," Truman said, "I am now in the position of a liar and a double crosser. I've never felt so in my life."[12]

Those third and fourth level State Department officials who tried to sabotage Truman's Middle East policy were also trying to block his anti-Soviet expansion programs. Truman had hoped to "clean them out" of the State Department, but he wasn't completely successful.[13] One wonders on what other occasions they managed to interfere with the President's foreign policy and what their motives were.

Clifford discovered that on March 16, Secretary Marshall directed Austin, on the recommendation of Arthur Lovett, to deliver his speech at the earliest appropriate moment. He also learned that the Secretary of State had made no provision to inform the President as to when the speech was to be delivered. In Clifford's handwriting, we find a memo dated 5/4/48 that described these developments:

> 3. Marshall to Austin March 16 - directs Austin to make speech. Marshall says Austin is to make speech as soon as possible as Austin believes appropriate.
> 4. Austin and Rusk were not instructed to delay speech until final vote in Security Council.
> 5. Marshall and Lovett left no word that President was to be informed when Austin was to speak.
> 6. Text of Austin's speech was not submitted to President for his approval.
> > A. It was the same substance as the draft previously submitted to President.

Disregarding Arab infiltration into Palestine, State Department officials insisted that "Jews in Palestine should be made to understand that they will receive no U.S. backing in case they persist in following a course of violence."[14]   On March 25, Truman issued a statement supporting Austin's speech: since Partition could not be carried out peacefully at present, the U.S. proposed a temporary trusteeship. This was not to be construed as "a substitution for the partition plan but as an effort to fill the vacuum soon to be created by the termination of the mandate on May 15."

Regardless of the U.S. reversal, the Jews of Erez Israel still planned to create the Jewish State. Moshe Shertok told Secretary Marshall that the Yishuv would fight indefinitely, even though it was "in desperate need of arms." Trusteeship, he said, was out of the question.[15]

Chaim Weizmann met with the U.S. delegation to the U.N. shortly after the policy change had been made. He asked what had brought about the change. Were they afraid of Soviet infiltration, an oil embargo or Arab military power? He reassured them that there was no grounds for such fears, that the Soviet Union could not establish a foothold in a Jewish State, that the Arabs needed to sell their oil to the West, and that Arab military strength was so disorganized that it should be assigned a factor of "zero."[16]

Austin's speech caused many to be disappointed with the United States, and with Harry S Truman in particular. Even Truman's good friends didn't know how to handle the situation.[17]

Truman's old friend Eddie Jacobson recalled that Dr. Weizmann had reassured him about the President's sincerity, and that he had faith in Truman. But in view of Weizmann's April 9, 1948 letter to Truman, one wonders if he kept that faith:

> Arabs believe that an international decision has been revised in their favor purely because they dared to use force against it. Mr. President, I cannot see how this belief can honestly be refuted. The practical question now is whether your Administration will proceed to leave our people unarmed in the face of an attack which it apparently feels it is unable to stop; and whether it can allow us to come directly or indirectly under Arab domination which is sworn to our destruction.
>
> The choice for our people, Mr. President, is between Statehood and extermination. History and providence have placed this issue in your hands, and I am confident that you will yet decide it in the spirit of the moral law.[18]

Jacobson told the President that the reversal had been "a terrible shock." He wanted to visit with Truman and talk the whole thing over, and "maybe we can work something out."[19]

Responding, Truman said that he had appreciated Eddie's letter "very much and sometime or other when we have an opportunity I'll sit down and discuss the situation.... My sole interest in that problem now is to stop the bloodshed and see if we can't work the matter out on a peaceful basis."[20]

Political sparks were flying when, on March 5, the U.N. Security Council adopted a resolution calling on "all governments and peoples" to prevent or reduce disorders from taking place in Palestine. The resolution had no effect, so on March 30 the United States introduced another resolution that asked "Arab and Jewish armed groups to cease acts of violence immediately." The Jewish Agency representatives opposed the U.S. resolution because it conveyed the impression that the fighting simply involved the population of Palestime and that Jews and Arabs were equally guilty. Moshe Shertok, the Jewish Agency representative, reminded the U.N. that Arab states had sent their forces into the fight. Before a truce could be accepted, Shertok insisted, Arab invaders had to leave Erez Israel. "No people anywhere in the world," he said, would "voluntarily sign a truce with invading forces converging upon it and posed to strike. This would not be a truce, it would be a capitulation."

Despite objections, the resolution was adopted by the Security Council. It did not, however, stop Arab states from continuing to send military units and equipment into Palestine. The State Department had detailed reports of "Arab irregular" forces invading Palestine. Some 16,000 troops had been recruited in Syria as of January 1, 1948, and the CIA documented that by February, 8,000 Arabs had slipped into Erez Israel from Syria, Lebanon and Trans-Jordan.[21] On April 16, the U.N. Security Council passed a third resolution again asking the belligerents to cease fighting, but this time the resolution also called on the neighboring Arab states to stop supplying the Arab guerilla units. The fighting continued.

On April 23, Samuel Rosenman telephoned good news to Dr. Weizmann: The President would recognize the new Jewish State as soon as it was proclaimed, but this information had to be kept absolutely secret.[22] While Truman secretly promised recognition, the State Department kept pressuring the Yishuv not to declare independence. Under Secretary of State Lovett threatened to expose Zionist activities and pressures exerted on behalf of the future Jewish State. He threatened to impose an embargo on dollars and oil as well as munitions. State Department officials wanted Arabs and Jews to meet at a round-table discussion in a Middle Eastern desert to examine their differences and work out an accord. One accord, suggested by Dean Rusk, who accused the Jews of "armed aggression," would have made a three-way split of Palestine with the northern half going to Syria and Trans-Jordan, the southern half going to Saudi Arabia, and the Jews receiving "a coastal state from Tel Aviv to Haifa."[23]

Moshe Shertok advised Marshall and Rusk that Palestinian Jews opposed the "somewhat spectacular proceeding" of a meeting in the desert,[24] and that they would "strenuously" oppose any prolongation of the British mandate, *de jure* or *de facto*.[25] Shertok tried to make it clear to Marshall that there could be no more postponement.[26]

But Dean Rusk still claimed that trusteeship was far more desirable. He argued that the Jews were in control of only one-third of the area of the Jewish State described in the November 29th U.N. resolution, and he preferred to seek a truce that excluded the proclamation of a Jewish State.[27] Rusk's call for a truce was one of at least two dozen expedients that American diplomats had tried in order to bring a Palestine settlement. Indeed, they had tried everything except consideration of a Jewish State, and the energy and time expended on equivocation was unprecedented. In the U.N. Security Council, U.S. diplomats had proposed that the Council carry out its responsibilities under the November 29 resolution if a threat to peace was involved; they proposed that a committee representing the world's five major powers develop a program to be presented to the Security Council; they proposed a temporary trusteeship for Palestine; they proposed a truce between Jews and Arabs. American diplomats proposed that a special session of the General Assembly consider the future of Palestine; that a truce commission composed of U.S., French and Belgian consuls be created in Jerusalem; and they tried to persuade Britain to agree to trusteeship and to furnish troops. Those same diplomats also worked to obtain British cooperation for a short extension of the mandate's life. Then the diplomats turned to the Jews and invited Dr. Judah Magnes, President of the Hebrew University and an opponent of the Jewish State, to meet with Truman; they tried to persuade the Jewish Agency to accept trusteeship; they tried to induce the Jewish Agency to agree to a ten day "stop-the-clock" truce with a temporary continuation of the British mandate; they tried to negotiate a ninety day truce; and they tried to dissuade the Jewish Agency from declaring a Jewish State after May 15. In addition, the State Department officials worked hard at enforcing an arms embargo and they sought to discourage all other countries from furnishing military supplies. And they tried to prevent underground Jewish immigration to the land of Israel.[28]

Partition was, however, an accomplished fact, and Clifford explained the circumstances to Truman on May 9. The British recognized this in reports from military commanders in Palestine and Egypt, as well as by their heavy investments in Jewish enterprises there, he said. The Jews had organized and maintained essential governmental services in their area of control, and they proclaimed their intention of confining the Jewish State to areas assigned them in the U.N. Partition Plan, even though they could have extended military control to other areas. The President had a choice, Clifford said - he could either recognize a Jewish State, or he could seek a reversal by using force, sanctions, threats or persuasion. But since those methods had not worked in the past, there was no reason to believe they could work in the future, Clifford argued, and by extending recognition, Truman could regain some of the prestige lost during previous weeks and months of equivocation. American prestige in the Arab world would likewise increase since the Arabs respected "reality rather than sentimentality." American prestige would also be enhanced *vis a vis* the Soviet Union. It was expected that the Soviets and their satellites would recognize the Jewish State and if they were the first to do so, American recognition might be regarded as "begrudging," and this "would represent a diplomatic defeat for the United States." At home, Republicans would be pressing Truman "before, during and after their convention" for recognition, but that could be eliminated from the Republican campaign provided Truman recognized the Jewish State before May 16.[29]

By May 12, 1948, Clifford received field reports that indicated the Jews could defend themselves. Major George Fielding Eliot, a writer for American papers, reported that the efficiency and strength which the Jewish Army had displayed in the field during the past weeks raised some very grave doubts as to whether a concerted invasion by all the Arab armies could be successful after May 15. Daniel DeLuce, of the Associated Press, reported that the Jewish State was a reality. Regardless of the grandiose communiques issued after each Arab conference, there were strong indications that the old jealousies among the Arab kings and premiers ran on unabated.[30]

Despite such optimistic evaluations, the Jewish position in Palestime during May 1948 was far from secure. They had few men and hardly enough equipment for facing the challenges of a well-armed group of enemies. According to recently published sources, the total number of men in the Haganah on May 14, 1948, was between 28,760 and 35,000. This included mobilized infantry, the home guard, air force, navy and special services groups. In terms of weaponry, they had 22,000 rifles, 11,000 sub-machine guns, 105 three-inch mortars, 682 two-inch mortars, 16 Davidkas, 75 Piats and anti-tank rifles, and four 65 mm artillery pieces. The Arabs had far more men, and substantially more equipment of every sort.[31]

Jewish leaders had expected supplies from the West, and with those supplies, they believed that they could succeed. But the supplies never came because of the Anglo-Arab blockade and the U.N. sponsored embargo. On April 17, 1948, the U.N. Security Council passed a resolution that imposed a general arms embargo, and a ban on immigrants of fighting age, in the Palestine area. While some U.N. members, such as the United States, observed the resolution, Britain continued to furnish arms to Egypt, Trans-Jordan and Iraq. Using the communist bogeyman threat, the British claimed that their treaty commitments required them to ship arms to the Arabs. Ambassador Inverchapel argued that unless the British provided arms, they would not be able to prevent internal disorders caused by communist subversives.[32] At the same time, the State Department was advising Truman against lifting the arms embargo. If the United States provided Jews with weapons, it would "evoke hostile and violent mob reactions against the U.S. and irreparably damage American-Arab relations." Moreover, it would "result in the destruction of American tactical and strategic security throughout the entire Near East...."[33] The Soviet Union and Czechoslovakia ignored the U.N. embargo resolution and sold arms to both Jews and Arabs.[34]

Chaim Weizmann wrote President Truman, suggesting that the United States, "the greatest living democracy be the first to welcome the newest into the family of nations." But Lovett and Marshall maintained that such a move would be "injurious to the Prestige of the President." Lovett accused Truman of trying to "win the Jewish vote" with recognition of the Jewish State. Clifford advised President Truman to recognize the Jewish State, but Lovett complained that Palestine was filled with "Jews and Communist agents from Black Sea area." Marshall bellowed that "if the President were to follow Mr. Clifford's advice...(he) would vote against the President" in the next election. Truman responded to all his advisors that he was fully aware of the difficulties and dangers of the situation and the political risks he would face.[35]

While Arab swords rattled and State Department officials prophesized an Armageddon, the Palestinian Jews asked the world to persuade the Arabs not to make further war. On May 13, 1948, Shertok telegraphed Truman: "Urge immediate strongest effort secure immediate direct sternest warning by President personally to King Abdullah."[36] The Jews asked Truman to urge Abdullah not to commit his armies to the conflict."Hours count," Shertok said.[37] Clifford asked Epstein, the Jewish Agency's representative, if the Jews were still determined to proclaim their independence. Epstein answered that there was not the slightest doubt. Clifford then asked him to draft a letter requesting U.S. recognition[38]. With the help of Benjamin V. Cohen, he drafted the following request.

> With full knowledge of the deep bond of sympathy which has existed and has been strengthened over the past 30 years between the Government of the U.S. and the Jewish people of Palestine. I have been authorized by the provisional government of the new state to tender this message and to express the hope that your government will recognize and will welcome Israel into the community of nations.

The letter was rushed to the White House and President Truman issued the following statement of recognition a few minutes after Israel proclaimed its independence:

> This Government has been informed that a Jewish state has been proclaimed in Palestine, and recognition has been requested by the provisional Government thereof.
> The United States recognizes the provisional government as the *de facto* authority of the new Jewish State of Israel.
>
> Harry Truman
> *(signed)*

Approved,
May 14, 1948.
6:11

At 5:45 p.m., Clifford called Rusk to tell him that President Truman would recognize Israel at 6 p.m. Rusk was opposed. He claimed that recognition would "cut across what our Delegation has been trying to accomplish in the General Assembly under instructions and we have a large majority for that approval." They were trying to accomplish another trusteeship under British control. "Nevertheless," insisted Clifford, "this is what the President wishes you to do."[39]

Rusk called Senator Austin, who was addressing the U.N. General Assembly. Austin left the rostrum to pick up the call, and when he heard of the President's decision, he refused to return to the General Assembly that day.[40] There was also some talk of resignation, but it was only talk.

Some of the State Department establishment expressed surprise with Truman's recognition of Israel. But if they had followed Truman's policies instead of trying to sabotage them, they wouldn't have been so surprised.

The Israelis quickly made Partition a reality, and recognition added to that reality by welcoming the new state into the family of nations. But while recognition was an important step towards Israeli independence, the road to peace and security was still a very long and difficult one. The Israelis would still have to face the continued opposition of State Department, British Foreign Office and Soviet Politburo establishments. They would have to overcome the jealousies of Arab neighbors who attempted to use Israel as a scapegoat for their own inadequacies. They would have to face Bernadotte plans, arms embargoes, British and Soviet intervention, the factionalism within Israeli society and the Diaspora.

Was Truman moved by righteousness? Perhaps.

He was also motivated by the reality of the situation and what he thought was best for the United States. Since the Soviet Union was seeking to advance its position in the Middle East, Truman wanted to make sure that they would not get a foothold in Israel. The Soviets were selling weapons to the Israelis, and they were more than willing to offer recognition. Truman, who had helped Turkey, Greece and Western Europe remain free of Soviet control, must have seen that U.S. recognition of Israel fell in line with his policies.[41] But recognition was not everything.

1 Margaret Truman, *Harry S Truman*, (New York, 1973) 388. Hereafter cited as M.Truman, *Harry S Truman*. According to Joseph P. Lash's recent biography of Eleanor Roosevelt, U.S. officials led by James Forrestal and Arthur Lovett, pressed for some form of trusteeship over Palestine. See Joseph P. Lash, *Eleanor: The Years Alone* (New York, 1972), 122-123. Hereafter cited as Lash, *Years Alone*. According to Rabbi Israel Goldstein, former President of the Zionist Organization of America, there were some Zionist leaders who were anxious for a trusteeship rather than war. Interview with Israel Goldstein, October 2, 1973.

2 M. Truman, *Harry S Truman*, 388.

3 Harry S Truman, *Years of Trial and Hope*, (New York, 1956), 164. Hereafter cited as Truman, *Years of Trial and Hope*. Interview with Emanuel Neumann, May 6, 1971.

4 *Foreign Relations of the United States 1948* (Washington, D.C., 1976) Volume V, Part 2, 549-561. Hereafter cited as *Foreign Relations Papers*.

5 *Ibid.*, 593-595.

6 Dan Kurzman, *Genesis 1948, The First Arab-Israeli War*, (New York, 1970) 84-86. M. Truman, *Harry S Truman*, 388.

7 *Foreign Relations Papers 1948*, 670-671.

8 M. Truman, *Harry S Truman*, 388.

9 Truman to Marshall, February 22, 1948, *Foreign Relations of the United States*, V, 2, 645.

10 Clark Clifford Memo, March 8, 1948, Clark Clifford Papers, Harry S Truman Library. *Foreign Relations Papers 1948*, V, 2, 687-696.

11 *Ibid.*

12 M. Truman, *Harry S Truman*, 388-389. That morning the Soviets called on the Arabs to withdraw their forces from Palestine. They demanded an end to the bloodshed and war brought on by the Arabs. *Foreign Relations Papers 1948*, V, 2, 732-735. According to one State Department official — Charles Bohlen — President Truman "was so much exercised in the matter" because "Austin made his statement without the President having been advised that he was going to make it at that particular time." But Bohlen seemed to be giving it the State Department "twist." C. Bohlen to Marshall, March 22, 1948, *Foreign Relations Papers 1948*, V, 2, 750.

13 M. Truman, *Harry S Truman*, 388-389.

14 *Foreign Relations Papers 1948*, V, 2, 756-757.

15 *Ibid.*, 762-763.

16 *Ibid.*, 821-824.

17 Lash, *Years Alone*, 130.

18 Chaim Weizmann to President Truman, April 9, 1948, Zionist Archives, New York City. The letter was filed away with the following notation: "Not answered RAC (Rose A. Conway, Administrative Assistant in the President's office)" OF 204 Misc, Truman Papers, Independence, Missouri, *Foreign Relations Papers 1948*, V, 2, 802-809.

19 Personal Papers of the President, File 1656, Harry S Truman Library.

20 *Ibid.*

When Weizmann died in 1952, President Truman wrote Jacobson as to how he felt about the first President of Israel:
"I felt as if I had lost a personal friend when he died. He and I have had some wonderful conversations on the world situation and the necessary remedies to meet conditions and maintain peace in the world.

"I wish he could have lived longer. It would have been a great benefit to his country and to all of the rest of us who are working for world peace."
— Harry S Truman to Eddie Jacobson, November 28, 1952, Eddie Jacobson Papers, Zionist Archives, New York.

But at the time of decisions in 1948, he might have considered some of the bare military facts he received from Defense Secretary Forrestal and Chief of Staff Leahy, both of whom were never very friendly to the Jews or to the Jewish State idea. Forrestal estimated that it would take 50,000 U.S. troops to keep the peace in the Middle East. This was "substantially" the "entire" U.S. ground reserve. No other troops would be available for deployment elsewhere until such time as the Selective Service draft came into effect. Leahy recommended that the U.K. furnish 48,000 troops and that France provide 10,400 of her own to keep the peace. *Foreign Relations Papers 1948*, V, 2, 798-800, 832-833.

21 *Ibid.*, 555-556, 671.

22 Kurzman, *Genesis 1948*, 212.

23 *Foreign Relations Papers 1948*, V, 2, 894-895; Kurzman, *Genesis 1948*, 212; Interview with Emanuel Neumann, May 6, 1971; Shertok to Rusk, May 4, 1948, Clark Clifford Papers, Harry S Truman Library; *Foreign Relations Papers 1948*, V, 2, 640-648. Every possible means was used by American officials to block the Zionist cause. Lovett invited the anti-Zionist Judah P. Magnes to Washington to speak against Zionism. President of Hebrew University, Magnes met with U.S. officials in May and spoke derogatively about the Jewish State. Time, said this Jewish academician, was on the side of the Arabs. He urged that the U.S. impose "financial sanctions" against both Jews and Arabs so as to bring an end to the fighting. He felt certain that "if contributions from the U.S. were cut off, the Jewish war machine in Palestine would come to a halt...." Only trusteeship was the answer. His views fit particularly well with the State Department establishment and the views of such groups as the American Jewish Committee at that time. *Foreign Relations Papers 1948*, V, 2, 901-904; Shertok to Rusk, May 4, 1948, Clark Clifford Papers, Harry S Truman Library.

24 *Ibid.*

25 *Ibid.*

26 *Ibid.*

27 Clifford Conversation with Rusk, May 6, 8, 1948, Clifford Papers, Harry S Truman Library.

28 Unsigned Memo to Clark Clifford, May 7, 1948, Clark Clifford Papers, Harry S Truman Library, Clark Clifford Memo, May 9, 1948, Clark Clifford Papers, Harry S Truman Library

30 *Ibid.*, May 12, 1948.

31 Kimche, *A Clash of Destinies*, 160-162.

32 *Foreign Relations Papers 1948*, V, 2, 581.

33 *Ibid.* 1060ff.

34 Kimche, *A Clash of Destinies,* 157.

35 *Foreign Relations Papers 1948,* V, 2, 972-977.

36 Clark Clifford Memo, May 13, 1948, Clifford Papers, Truman Library.

37 *Foreign Relations Papers 1948,* V, 2, 972-977.

38 *Ibid.,* 959.

29 *Ibid.,* 1005-1007.

40 *Ibid.,* 993.

41 H. Druks, *Harry S Truman and The Russians* (New York, 1967).

Chapter III

Recognition Was Not Everything

Trusteeship was out of the question and Israel had to fight for its own survival. The armies of Egypt, Syria, Trans-Jordan and Iraq, reinforced with troops and equipment from a half-dozen other Arab states, mobilized against the new Jewish State while the Secretary General of the Arab League proclaimed:

> This will be another war of extermination which will be talked about like the Mongol massacres and the Crusades.[1]

The Arabs wanted all of Erez Israel, but each Arab faction had its own objectives, and sometimes these conflicted. King Abdullah of Trans-Jordan wanted to extend his desert kingdom to the Mediterranean and was particularly interested in the Haifa area and the Negev. Syria wanted northern Palestine. The Mufti of Jerusalem, a Nazi collaborator, wanted to liquidate the Jews. While Iraq and Syria made several serious threats, neither was truly prepared for intervention. And although Egypt and Saudi Arabia were preoccupied with domestic difficulties, they were also apprehensive over Abdullah's expansionist desires, and opted for intervention.

U.N. Secretary General Lie observed that Egypt was trying "to establish a *de facto* position beyond its frontiers" and if this was not stopped, "the future usefulness of both the United Nations and its Security Council" would be prejudiced.[2] Two days after Egyptian forces invaded the Jewish State, the U.N. Security Council met to consider a U.S. cease-fire proposal. But British Ambassador Sir Alexander Cadogan rejected the measure, saying that there had been no clear case of aggression.

36

A week later, on May 22, the United States again claimed that there had been a breach of peace in the Middle East, and once again proposed a cease-fire. Again, the British rejected the proposal. The Israelis were prepared to accept these cease-fire efforts, but blocking efforts by Britain and Syria managed to keep the olive leaf off the U.N. discussion table.

On May 29, the Soviet Union proposed, with U.S. and French support, a "cease-fire within 36 hours under threat of U.N. sanctions;" but the British veto power blocked this too. Instead, the British offered their own cease-fire resolution that obviated any U.N. sanction against the Arabs. This resolution passed on May 30, the day Old Jerusalem fell to the Arabs. The resolution called upon all belligerents to accept a four week truce, and if this was rejected, repudiated or violated, the U.N. was to take action authorized by the U.N. Charter. By the time the cease-fire went into effect on June 11, more than a third of the land allocated to the Jewish State by the U.N. had fallen into Arab hands.

Britain pretended neutrality, but sustained the Trans-Jordanian Arab Legion with guns, money and officers. It was British advisers who briefed Egyptian pilots before they took off for bombing missions over Israel, and it was the British who dispatched some 3,000 Sudanese troops to assist the Arab Legion. In effect, the British used the Arabs as their proxy in their war against Israel.[3]

Why were the British trying so hard to see Israel destroyed? According to Clark Clifford, the British were searching desperately for allies in the Arab world and they hoped to win this friendship by helping to destroy the Jews.[4]

Despite all their spirit and courage, the Israelis were in bad shape. Representatives of the Jewish State wired President Truman on July 1, 1948, for some desperately needed supplies: "...rush at least one hundred tons of milk powder and fifty tons of egg powder to Jerusalem before July 9." And the Israelis were ready to pay for these relief supplies with their own funds.[5]

The situation was well summarized in a letter a Jerusalem Jew sent to his brother in America on August 16, 1948:

Dear Brother,
    We received your letter of July 20, 1948, and we wondered that you took such a long time to ask what we are doing here. It is hard to describe all that we have suffered during this time. It is enough that we

are still alive.   Our apartment was <u>bombarded</u> and we are almost inundated by the attacks. We barely saved our lives. We suffered very much from hunger and thirst and the end is not yet near. All night long there was shooting in the city. The artillery barrage was heavy and we have no roof over our heads now.

The mail comes from America regularly. Some folks received weekly packages of food from America.

Nourishment here is defective and faulty. There is a shortage of all essentials including flour, meat, eggs and milk. But what is worst of all, is the shortage of drinking water. Nobody dreams of washing himself because of this water shortage. The heat becomes greater and greater.

Our so-called Socialist political leaders have obtained their objectives. They are ministers and ambassadors of a Jewish State without Jerusalem and without a Land.

Tel Aviv suffered a great deal, but only from the air attacks. My son Oscar is not doing well. He has no job and our situation is poor. During the whole time of this war it was still possible to write to Tel Aviv.

How goes it with you and your family? Is your son studying well?

Because of hunger and fear, our health has deteriorated greatly. Hopefully God will help and our difficulties will lessen.

Do not expect any further letters from us, but write often. Be healthy and strong.

With kisses and best wishes from,

Ever yours,
Shlomo and Malca

Shlomo would not make it through that war, nor would six thousand other Jews.

THE LOAN TO ISRAEL

A loan to Israel promised by the United States was very slow in coming. On May 25, 1948, President Truman assured Chaim Weizmann that Israel would have no difficulty in getting a substantial loan for construction purposes. But after several months and a great many explanations as to what the money would be used for, Israel still had no loan. One reason it took so long was because State Department officials wanted to use the loan as leverage to force Israel into making territorial concessions to the Arabs.

On July 29, the Israeli representative to Washington went to see the President. Truman again expressed great interest in the resettlement of displaced persons and related economic developments. But by August 3, there still was no loan. Ambassador Elath then wrote to Clifford. Did the President know ''how repeatedly we have been put off on this matter, from week to week, and from month to month?"[6]

The loan was finally approved on the day that the United States extended *de jure* recognition to Israel. That was January 31, 1949.

THE BERNADOTTE PLAN

Even after recognition, and after the Israeli forces had proven themselves in the field as being capable of mounting a viable defense, there were still concerted efforts to reverse history and dismiss Israel from reality. One such effort, sponsored by British and U.S. diplomats, was the Bernadotte Plan.

Swedish Count Folke Bernadotte was appointed as U.N. Mediator in Palestine on May 20, 1948, by the Security Council. Britain interpreted this as a mandate for the Mediator to seek some solution other than Partition, and Bernadotte seemed to accept that interpretation. On May 25, before Bernadotte had time to establish himself in his new Parisian office, British Charge d'Affaires Ashley Clark paid him a visit to inform him that Great Britain was not prepared to accept any sanctions imposed against the Arabs. Bernadotte was also told that the British were continuing to supply the Arabs with military hardware and that their military advisors were actively participating in the war. Moreover, Clark informed him that Britain wanted to put the Negev under Trans-Jordan's control since its only practical use was to serve as a land link between Arab capitals.[7]

Bernadotte felt that it would have been better if a unitary state had been established in Palestine "with far-reaching rights for the Jews." But as the Jews started to have military success, and there could be no return to former situations, Bernadotte started thinking about border modifications. On June 27, 1948, the Mediator made the following recommendations for Palestine:

> The right of residents of Palestine to return to their places of abode without restrictions on their rights to regain possession of their property.
> Inclusion of the whole or part of the Negev in Arab territory.
> Inclusion of the whole or part of the Western Galilee in Jewish territory.
> Inclusion of the City of Jerusalem in Arab territory, with municipal autonomy for the Jewish community and special arrangements for the protection of the Holy places.
> Establishment of a free port at Haifa.
> Establishment of a free port at Lydda.

Thus, according to the Bernadotte Plan, the Negev would be given to the Arabs while the Western Galilee region would go to the Jews. Israel was to become part of a dual state, to be joined in a union with Jordan, and Jerusalem (with its Jewish majority) was to be in Trans-Jordanian hands, while the seaport of Haifa and the airport of Lydda were to become free ports. As a final blow to the concept of Israeli independence, immigration was to be determined by both parts of the dual state. Bernadotte felt that "unrestricted immigration" into Palestine might cause "serious economic and political problems beyond the control of any Jewish Government. It cannot be ignored that immigration affects not only the Jewish State and the Jewish people but also the surrounding Arab world." While he admitted that Jerusalem was of great concern to the Jews, Bernadotte insisted that the city "was never intended to be part of the Jewish State." He believed Jerusalem was a separate question from that of "the boundaries of a Jewish State."

Israel rejected Bernadotte's plan. It "noted with surprise" his suggestions that ignored the Resolution of the General Assembly of November 29, 1947, which still was "the only internationally valid adjudication of the question of the future government of Palestine." Israel found it regrettable that Bernadotte had not "taken into account the outstanding facts of the situation in Palestine, namely, the effective establishment of the sovereign State of Israel within the area assigned to it in the 1947 Resolution, and other territorial changes which have resulted from the repulse of the attack launched against the State of Israel by Palestinian Arabs and by the Governments of neighboring Arab States." As for Jerusalem, "Israel and the Jews of Jerusalem will never acquiesce in the imposition of Arab domination over Jerusalem....They will resist any such imposition with all the force at their command."

Israel also rejected the suggestion that immigration should be restricted. There was to be "complete and unqualified freedom to determine the size and composition of Jewish immigrants." Peace, insisted the Israelis, could be achieved only "as a result of an agreement negotiated between the interested parties as free and sovereign States."

Bernadotte was shot to death in Jerusalem on September 17, 1948, just as the U.N. General Assembly opened its doors to examine his plan, and the Israelis were very concerned that they would have to

Those terrorists become the leaders for Aparthied Israel.

pay for the actions of a few terrorists. Those fears seemed particularly warranted when various speakers at the U.N. urged that the Bernadotte plan be adopted as recognition for his work. Acting Mediator Ralph Bunche announced from his headquarters at Rhodes that he not only endorsed the plan, but he accused Israeli officials of having failed to provide adequate care for the safety of U.N. personnel. The U.S. Ambassador to Israel cabled home on September 17: "Regret report Count Bernadotte, U.N. observer Jerusalem and Colonel Serat, French officer, killed this afternoon...."[8]

A week later, Marshall announced his support of the Bernadotte Plan. The Secretary of State said that he found the Count's report "a generally fair basis for settlement of the Palestine question." He "strongly urged the parties concerned and the General Assembly to accept them in their entirety as the best possible basis for bringing peace to a distracted land."[9]

It seemed as if the United States was abandoning Israel. Chaim Weizmann asked Eddie Jacobson to remind the President how important the Negev was to the future of the Jewish State since it was suitable for immigration *to a desert* and was presently uninhabitable. Unless Israel received the Negev, it would remain a desert and a region from which Israel would be constantly attacked. Israel had already proven how it could bring agriculture to the sands of the Negev. "Please go and see him without delay and remind him of Democratic pledge that no changes in boundaries would take place without consent Government of Israel but above all his own encouragement to me on which we all implicitly rely and for which we shall be eternally grateful."[10]

On September 29, President Truman and his staff prepared a statement which was to be issued October 1, reaffirming U.S. support for Israel. At the same time, the following memo was prepared for Secretary Marshall's attention:

To: Secretary Marshall, Paris
From: The President   September 29, 1948

Your statement that the Bernadotte report should be used as a basis for negotiation in the settlement of the Palestine question requires clarification.

The government of the United States is on record as having endorsed the action of the United Nations General Assembly of November 1947 as to boundaries. As President I have so stated officially. The Democratic Platform endorsed the findings of the General Assembly.

I shall have to state that my position as to boundaries has not changed.
You should know that my statement will be made on October first.

To be sent immediately
Copy to Ast. Sec. Lovett, Washington

Truman wrote in his memoirs that when Marshall returned from Paris on October 9, he talked to him about the matter. Marshall claimed that his observations on the Bernadotte Plan had been made primarily to encourage negotiations between the Arabs and Israelis. He seemed to have been satisfied that Marshall understood his position and found that it was not necessary to issue a prepared statement.[11] But on October 29, 1948, during the election campaign, Truman publicly scotched the unrealistic Bernadotte Plan and declared that "Israel must be large enough, free enough, and strong enough to make its people self-supporting and secure."

The U.N. Security Council, with British and U.S. backing, imposed cease-fires whenever the Israelis started to gain victories, and the Israelis soon realized that in order to defend their new state, every military action would have to be well-planned and swift. When the second cease-fire expired on October 10, 1948, the Israelis were ready to strike back at the Arab invaders with lightning assaults concentrated in the Negev and Central Galilee. In the Galilee, the Israelis broke through the Arab armies and quickly cleared the entire area as far as the Litani River in Lebanon.

Meanwhile, David Ben Gurion desperately wanted to see Jerusalem established as the Israeli capital and devised a plan to open the city by sending Israeli troops to its south, cutting the Jordanian Arab Legion from direct contact with their Egyptian allies in the Negev. On September 26, Ben Gurion presented the plan to his Cabinet, but it was voted down. In his diary, the Israeli Prime Minister wrote: "The plan has been dropped. Fortunately for us, most of the offensives we've launched this year were not put to the vote of that lot!"[12]

Israel's next effort was directed at driving the Egyptians from the Negev. During the cease-fire, the Egyptians had refused to abide by the truce agreement that permitted Israel to send supply convoys through Egyptian lines to isolated Israeli units. Israeli intelligence also furnished information that, if hostilities broke out, no Arab armies would be in a position to help the Egyptians, so on October 15, a supply column was ordered south to test the Egyptian willingness to defy the truce accord. As expected, the Egyptians attacked it. And Israel was ready. *Operation Jacob* had begun.

Although the Israeli troops struck swiftly, international politicians showed that they too were capable of rapid action. As Israeli troops were about to liberate the Hebron-Bethlehem area, Great Britain threatened intervention and Ben Gurion ordered his troops to halt. As the Egyptians had been forced out of this area, it was soon reoccupied by Jordanian troops.

Meanwhile, the Israelis were intent on opening the route to the Negev by breaking the Arab salient at Falouja, a pocket which served as an Arab stepping stone between Gaza and the Hebron area. A pincer attack cut Falouja on both sides and effectively isolated it. Pleased with the success against the Egyptians, Ben Gurion then wanted to strike at the Iraqi forces in the triangle and mop up the remaining Arab forces that threatened to cut the Negev from the rest of Israel.

But first, he waited for world reaction to the offensive in the Negev. While Marshall visited Greece and Italy, the President instructed his U.N. delegation not to make any statements or take any action "on the subject of Palestine" without "specific" authorization "from me and clearing the text of any statement."

Ben Gurion then ordered an attack against the Egyptian troops in the south. One force hit the isolated Falouja pocket and another opened a road to the Dead Sea. Israeli guerilla activity coordinated with a rapid military attack, shattered the Egyptian defenses south of Beersheva.

Exploiting the victory, Israeli troops pressed on and crossed the border into Sinai on December 28. Abu Ageila, a main crossroads in Sinai, fell to the attack force, as did Bir-Hassne and Bir-Gafgafa. Advance Israeli troops halted about forty miles from Suez which, at the time, was still under British protection.

The main Israeli attack swung to the northwest and was posed to capture the Sinai capital of El-Arish, and another unit was ready to roll into Gaza through its Sinai back door, when Ben Gurion ordered withdrawal. This came because pressure from Great Britain and especially the United States, was too much to bear.

It was Great Britain that called on the United States to stop the Israeli Sinai campaign. On December 30, 1948, the British informed Acting Secretary of State Lovett that unless "the Jews withdrew from Egyptian territory'' the British would have to intervene on the basis of their 1936 treaty obligations with Egypt. They threatened ''the gravest possible consequences, not only to Anglo-American strategic interests in the Near East, but to American relations with Britain and Western Europe.'' As an aside, throughout the discussions, the British representatives seemed unable or unwilling to use the term *Israel*, but always used the term *the Jews* to describe Israel. They threatened to send supplies to the Arabs if Israel did not do as Great Britain wished. Hypocritically, they pretended that they had not been sending supplies to the Arabs.[13]   On December 31, Ben Gurion received the following threatening communication from the United States:

> The U.S. Government, which was the first to recognize the State of Israel and which is supporting its application to join the U.N., wishes to draw the attention of the Israeli Government to a fact that its attitude could endanger peace in the Middle East. The U.S. Government would have to re-examine its attitude with regard to the Israeli Government's application to join the U.N., which is presented as the application of a 'peace loving' nation, and would also have to re-examine the character of its relations with the State of Israel.[14]

As proof of Israel's peaceful intentions, the United States expected Israeli forces ''to withdraw immediately from Egyptian territory.'' On receipt of the communication, Ben Gurion informed the U.S. Ambassador that the withdrawal order had already been issued and that Israel had not violated the peace in Palestine. It had been the Arab armies in their invasion of Israel that had violated the peace. Ben Gurion wondered why the United States, a powerful nation, should choose to address Israel, ''a small and weak'' nation, in such tones.

The American communication had also asked about a report that Israel had demanded a peace treaty with Jordan and had threatened continued warfare unless there was such a treaty. If that was the case, the U.S. threatened, it ''would have no other course than to undertake a review of its attitude toward Israel.''[15]   The Israeli Foreign Minister assured McDonald that no threat of ''peace or war'' had been made to Trans-Jordan, but that in a secret meeting on December 30, Colonel Dayan and Mr. Shiloah met with King Abdullah in East Jerusalem offering to press negotiations further than a cease-fire. The Israelis wanted an armistice that would lead to peace.

The United States, supporting Britain, forced Israel to withdraw from Sinai. But meanwhile, an Israeli task force established a strong wedge south of Rafah near the Israeli-Egyptian border, and cut the Gaza Strip from Egypt. At this point, Egypt agreed to armistice negotiations, provided the Israeli troops were withdrawn from the Rafah area. Israel withdrew and, on February 29, 1949, an armistice was signed with Egypt and the Egyptians were permitted to retain control of the Gaza area.[16]

Had the United States and Britain not intervened to halt Israeli military operations, the geo-political situation for Israel would have been far more secure. As a result of their meddling, Gaza was turned over to Egypt, and Jordan gained control of a triangle of territory that included Jerusalem and jutted into Israel like a sharp knife threatening the jugular vein.

1 John and David Kimche, *Clash of Destinies* (New York, 1960), 49.

2 Clark Clifford Memos dated May 29, 31, 1948, Clark Clifford Papers, Harry S Truman Library.

3 *Ibid.*

4 *Ibid.*

5 Elath to President Harry S Truman, July 1, 1948, Clark Clifford Papers, Harry S Truman Library.

6 Elath to Clark Clifford, August 3, 1948, Clark Clifford Papers, Harry S Truman Library.

7 Count Folke Bernadotte, *To Jerusalem*, (London, 1951), 6-10.

8 James McDonald to State Department, September 17, 1948, Clark Clifford Papers, Harry S Truman Library.

9 *The New York Times,* September 22, 1948.

10 Chaim Weizmann to Eddie Jacobson, Telegram, September 1948, Clark Clifford Papers, Harry S Truman Library.

11 Truman, *Years of Trial and Hope,* 167.

12 Bar Zohar, *Ben Gurion: The Armed Prophet* (New Jersey, 1968) 150.

13 *Foreign Relations of the United States 1948,* (Washington, D.C., 1976), Vol. V, Part 2, December 30, 1948, 1703.

14 *Ibid.,* 1705.

15 *Ibid.*

16 Armistice agreements would be signed with Lebanon on March 23, 1949, Trans-Jordan on April 3, 1949, and Syria on July 20, 1949. Iraq withdrew from Trans-Jordan without signing an armistice with Israel.

Chapter IV

The 1948 Campaign and Israel

While President Truman had to face such challenges as the war between Israel and the Arabs, as well as the Soviet blockade of Berlin, Soviet expansionism in Europe and a civil war in China, he also had to campaign for re-election.

Although he tried to keep foreign affairs out of the campaign, the Republicans wouldn't let him. The Grand Old Party was anxious to put Thomas E. Dewey, its candidate, into the White House, and they used every possible device to achieve this goal. Republican leaders tried to discredit Truman's stand on Israel. John Foster Dulles and Thomas E. Dewey met with Zionist leaders on July 28, 1948, and promised them everything: full recognition of Israel, an end to the arms embargo, and a substantial loan. All they would have to do was support the Republican candidate. The GOP would attack Truman regardless of what he did. If the President would override Marshall on the Bernadotte Plan, the Republicans would accuse Truman of weakness. If Truman failed to overrule his Secretary of State, then Republicans, helped by some British officials, would blast the President for lacking ability and diplomacy.

By October 1948, candidate Dewey planned to issue a strong statement against the Bernadotte Plan. Bartley Crum (of the Anglo-American Committee days) and Bob Howard McGrath (Democratic National Chairman) advised Truman to speak out in favor of *de jure* recognition, the Israeli borders, and the $100 million loan, before Dewey could make his speech.[1] But Truman did not follow their advice. He still hoped to keep foreign affairs out of partisan politics. On the occassion of the Jewish New Year, Truman issued a public statement to Israel's President: "May the New Year bring peace to

Israel and to its citizens the opportunity to dedicate themselves in tranquility to furthering the prosperity of their country.''

On October 22, Dewey issued his statement repudiating Truman's policies without committing himself to full support of Israel. He called for aid to Israel and full recognition of the Jewish State and its boundaries as sanctioned by the U.N. vote. But he failed to specify which U.N. vote, that of November 1947, or some future decision.[2] Since Dewey declared that President Truman had gone back on the Democratic platform promises, Truman issued the following statement on October 24, 1948:

> So that everyone may be familiar with my position, I set out here the Democratic Platform on Israel:
>
> "President Truman, by granting immediate recognition to Israel, led the world in extending friendship and welcome to a people who have long sought and justly deserve freedom and independence.
>
> "We pledge full recognition of the State of Israel. We affirm our pride that the United States, under the leadership of President Truman, played a leading role in the adoption of the resolution of November 29, 1947, by the United Nations General Assembly for the creation of a Jewish state.
>
> "We approve the claims of the State of Israel to the boundaries set forth in the United Nations' resolution of November 29 and consider that modifications thereof should be made only if fully acceptable to the State of Israel.
>
> "We look forward to the admission of the State of Israel to the United Nations and its full participation in the international community of nations. We pledge appropriate aide to the State of Israel in developing its economy and resources.
>
> "We favor the revision of the arms embargo to accord the State of Israel the right of self-defense. We pledge ourselves to work for the modification of any resolution of the United Nations to the extent that it may prevent any such revision.
>
> "We continue to support, within the framework of the United Nations, the internationalization of Jerusalem and the protection of the holy places in Palestine.''

Four days later, President Truman attacked Dewey for bringing foreign policy issues into the arena of domestic politics. ''The subject of Israel,'' Truman insisted, ''must not be resolved as a matter of politics in a political campaign. I have refused, first, because it is my responsibility to see that our policy in Israel fits in with our foreign policy throughout the world; second, it is my desire to help build in Palestine a strong, prosperous, free and independent democratic state. It must be large enough, free enough, and strong enough to make its people self-supporting and secure." With or without Dewey's prodding, Truman aimed to fulfill the pledges of the Democratic Platform, and according to the following undated Truman memo, he wanted U.S. officials involved with Israel to carry out those pledges:

> *Recognition:* Truman wanted full and complete *de jure* recognition announced "at least one week before the opening of the meeting of the General Assembly in Paris."
> *Boundaries:* He approved the boundaries established in the U.N. resolution of November 29, and he intended to stress Israel's boundary claims.
> *Admission to the U.N.:* He assumed that the U.S. would "actively and unconditionally sponsor the admission of the State of Israel to the U.N. at the forthcoming meeting of the General Assembly at Paris."
> *Aid to Israel:* As the $100 million loan to Israel was still pending, he wondered if there was any way to "expedite prompt favorable action upon this application?" He also wanted to know if there was any other appropriate aid which could be rendered "within the framework of existing legislation?"
> *Arms Embargo:* The President called for a revision of the arms embargo and he wanted to know "to what extent do any resolutions of the U.N. now prevent such revision, and, if so, what prompt action can we take to work for their modification?"
> *Jerusalem:* He supported the internationalization of Jerusalem and protection of Holy Places in the area.[3]

According to this memorandum, President Truman aimed to carry out his campaign pledges and he asked each official and employee involved with the questions to put their opinions into writing if he planned to conform "conscientiously and effectively" with the Democratic platform. Moreover, he called for the "immediate rearrangement of any such official or employee who does not unqualifiedly answer in the affirmative, so that he will not deal with any aspect of our policy or action concerning Israel." Truman wanted the names of such individuals by November, and he wanted written notification of any actions inconsistent with the Democratic platform.

After Truman was re-elected, he wrote Weizmann again, promising *de jure* recognition:

> I was struck by one common experience you and I recently shared. We had both been abandoned by the so-called realistic experts to our supposedly forelorn lost causes. Yet we both kept pressing for what we were sure was right — and we were both proven right. My feelings of

elation on the morning of November 3rd must have approximated your own feelings one year ago today, and on May 14th, and on several occasions since then.

However, it does not take long for bitter and resourceful opponents to regroup their forces after they have been shattered. You in Israel have already been confronted with that situation, and I expect to be all too soon. So I understand very well your concern to prevent the undermining of your well-earned victories.

I remember well our conversation about the Negev, to which you referred in your letter. I agree fully with your estimate of the importance of that area to Israel, and I deplore any attempt to take it away from Israel. I had thought that my position should have been clear to all the world, particularly in the light of the specific wording of the Democratic Party Platform. But there were those who did not take this seriously, regarding it as "just another campaign promise" to be forgotten after the election. I believe they have recently realized their error. I have interpreted my re-election as a mandate from the American people to carry out the Democratic Platform — including, of course, the plank on Israel. I intend to do so.

I was pleased to learn that the first Israeli elections have been scheduled for January 25th. That enables us to set a definite target date for extending *de jure* recognition.[4]

U.N. ADMISSION

As Israel celebrated the first anniversary of the passage of the U.N. Palestine Partition Plan, it presented Secretary General Lie with a formal application for U.N. membership. A few days later, both U.S. and Soviet delegates to the world body joined in calling the admission of Israel "as a matter of urgency." British and French delegates objected and called for a postponement, but this attempt was defeated. In the Security Council, the United States and the Soviet Union favored Israeli admission, as did Argentina, Columbia and the Ukraine. Syria voted in opposition; and Belgium, Canada, Great Britain, China and France abstained. The application failed to receive a majority vote in the Security Council and the measure was rejected.

After the Israeli-Egyptian armistice of February 24, 1949, Israel again applied for membership in the United Nations. This time, the application was accepted by a wide margin with nine votes in favor, one opposed (Egypt) and one abstention (Great Britain). The application was then put before the General Assembly for ratification.

Just as the General Assembly's Political Committee was to vote on

Israeli admission, Dean Rusk called on Elath to complain that Abba Eban had not explained what concessions Israel was prepared to make on the Arab refugee question and on frontiers. Rusk warned that unless Israel was prepared to make concession, its admission to the United Nations would be rejected. But Israel did not yield to the State Department pressures. When the Political Committee voted, Israel received more than a two-thirds vote and the question was then placed on the agenda of the Plenary Session for the next day, May 11, 1949. After that successful vote, Israel was admitted as a sovereign member of the United Nations.

An Overview

President Truman was known as a man of decision. But before he made his decisions, he considered the issues most carefully. This was the case when he decided to drop the atomic bombs on Japan, to confront Soviet expansionism in Europe and Asia, and this was the case with respect to his policy toward Israel. He felt deeply for his fellow human beings, and he was a man of courageous decisiveness and impeccable honesty.

His decision to recognize Israel came only after long and careful consideration. In 1946, Truman urged the British to admit 100,000 Jews to Palestine and he fought for a revision of U.S. immigration laws. But he was not willing to send American troops, nor was he willing to go beyond the limitations of the immigration laws through executive decrees, as Eisenhower would do in 1956. He supported the plan to Partition Palestine in 1947 but, for a time, he did not prevent his Secretary of State from advocating the Bernadotte Plan which would have transferred the Negev to the Arabs.

President Truman extended *de facto* recognition to Israel in response to the reality of the time. Israel had proclaimed independence, and the Soviet Union supported her. Truman had no wish to see the Soviets establish bases there and, regardless of what the old guard State Department and Defense Department establishment may have had against the Jewish State, Truman extended his recognition. He would not tolerate any potential for the breeding of Soviet influence in Israel. Truman's prime concern was for the welfare of the United States, and with that in mind, he sought to help freedom-loving states maintain their independence. Israel was one such state.

The study of Truman's policy towards Israel is interesting not only because it reveals how a President made his decisions, but it also shows how difficult it was for a President to overcome opposition from within his own administration even after policy goals had been set. First, Truman had to ascertain the facts, and this was not easy to do because Arabs, Arabists and Jews bombarded him with many conflicting statistics, pressures and proposals. State and Defense department officials, many of whom were leftovers from Franklin Roosevelt's administration, repeatedly cautioned him against supporting the Jews and urged him to side with the Arabs. Then, once he decided upon his policy of support for Israel, some officials tried to sabotage it. Ambassador Austin's speech at the U.N. in favor of trusteeship defied Truman's support of Partition. Secretary Marshall's support of the Bernadotte Plan which surrendered the Negev to the Arabs, reversed Truman's repeated assertions that the Negev should be part of Israel. Truman had a tough job keeping his own house in order as well as meeting outside challenges. But he met both problems head-on and handled them well.

The period after the proclamation of the Jewish State was a terribly difficult time for Israel. Israelis faced the threat of annihilation, and they were keenly aware of this threat because six million Jews had been murdered only a few years before by Nazi Germany. The Israelis also realized that they had no great friends in the Western world. Indeed, states such as Britain and the U.S. had refused to accept Jewish refugees from the Holocaust, and they collaborated to close Palestine to Jewish immigration. To keep peace with the Arabs, they pandered to the violently anti-Jewish sentiments of the pro-Nazi Mufti of Jerusalem.

The London Government supplied the Arab armies with British officers, training, guns, tanks, aircraft, money, intelligence information and, until May 15, 1948, worked tirelessly at keeping Jewish survivors of the Nazi inferno from entering Israel. The Arab armies descended on the Jewish State, and the Jews had only one option — they had to fight back.

The Jews did fight, and they fought hard. Unlike the European Jews of a decade before, the Israelis built their own army and organized a unified plan of operations. While the European Jews only confronted the Nazis during isolated incidents, the Israelis were united and determined to meet every Arab attack.

Harry Truman helped Israel through recognition, but his adherence to the U.N.'s Middle East arms embargo made the physical defense of the Jewish State very difficult. Only the Soviet Union and

Czechoslovakia openly sold weapons to Israel. Any arms obtained from the U.S. were procured *sub rosa*.

Complete *de jure* recognition was not granted by President Truman until after Israel conducted its first election on January 25, 1949. Truman apparently wanted to see if Israel would conduct internal politics democratically. The Soviet Union, however, extended immediate *de jure* recognition. The loan of $100 million, which Israel had requested in 1948, and which the Democrats and Republicans had talked about through the 1948 election, was not provided until January 31, 1949.

The man from Missouri had moments of hesitation when it came to the question of Israel, but he did support the new State and he saw great hope for the people of the entire Middle East. He envisioned Israel as a beacon that would help stimulate economic and industrial growth throughout that part of the world. Through his Truman Doctrine, the Marshall Plan and Point-Four self-help programs, he provided aid to all nations that were prepared to help themselves. As he put it to me in 1962, the United States had sent a team of Tennessee Valley Authority engineers and scientists to advise the Iraqi Government on how to develop the Tigris and Euphrates rivers. Those experts came up with a plan to develop the region so it could sustain 60 million people, but the Iraqis failed to accept the plan.

"The plan is in my library," Truman said. "They can have it for free. All they have to do is come and take it."[6]

Those such as Richard H. Nolte,[7] the former U.S. Ambassador to Egypt, and former Senator William Fulbright, who maintained that Israel obtained whatever it wanted from the United States, did not know the history of the U.S. and Israel during the Truman years. And for that matter, they seemed to know little about the difficult years that followed.

1 Bartley Crum to Clark Clifford, Telegram, October 3, 1948, Clark Clifford Papers, Harry S Truman Library.

2 J.S. Keenan to M.J. Connelly, October 23, 1948, Clark Clifford Papers, Harry S Truman Library.

3 Harry S Truman Memorandum, undated, Presidential Papers, Harry S Truman Library.

4 Papers of Clark Clifford, Harry S Truman Library.

5 Robert St. John, *Eban*, (New York, 1972), 219-221.

6 Interview with President Harry S Truman, August 2, 1962.

7 Interview with Richard H. Nolte, March 19, 1970.

Chapter V

The 1956 War

After the armistices were concluded in 1949, some believed that peace might be achieved. But there was no peace. Insisting upon a return to the 1947 boundaries and the repatriation of 500,000 to 750,000 Arab "refugees" the Arab states refused to acknowledge the existence of the State of Israel, and they continued to use Israel as a hate target to maintain unity within their own borders. Moreover, they imposed economic boycotts against Israel and barred Israeli shipping through the Suez Canal and the Gulf of Eilat despite U.N. recommendations that Israeli shipping be permitted passage. A few days after truces were concluded between Israel and her Arab neighbors, the Arabs inaugurated their murderous attacks upon Israeli civilians. These terrorist bands, or *Fedayeen,* organized and equipped by Egypt, Syria, Jordan and Lebanon, spread their terror throughout Israel by looting, bombing and murdering men, women and children.

From 1949 to 1953, 175 Jews were killed and 282 wounded in 1,182 incursions from Jordan. Those attacks reached a climax during the first half of October, 1953. On October 14, Israel retaliated by sending a paramilitary force into Jordan. The Mixed Armistice Commission reported to the Security Council that 53 Arab men, women and children had been killed and 15 wounded in the village of Kibya. The Security Council took up the Kibya case on November 24, 1953, and approved a resolution sponsored by the U.S., Britain and France which strongly censured Israel, adding the admonishment to "take effective measures to prevent all such such actions in the future." The resolution contained only slight reference to Jordanian crossings into Israel. It was a one-sided condemnation. The Security Council consistently refused to differentiate between cause and effect, provocation and reaction. The U.S. would time and time again respond to Arab complaints by supporting resolutions of censure condemning Israel, but Israeli complaints seldom received support.[1]

After the Kibya retaliatory raid, Israel proposed a review of the Armistice Agreement with Jordan in accordance with Article XII of that understanding which stipulated that if either party would ask the Secretary General of the U.N. to call a meeting with the other party to reconsider or revive the agreement, attendance was mandatory. Secretary General Hammarskjold asked Jordan to meet with Israel, but Jordan refused. Thus, the Security Council was inhibited by Soviet vetoes; the Mixed Armistice Commission was impotent; and Jordan refused revision. Israel had nothing left but to stop the Arabs through deterrent actions.[2]

From the Fall of 1954, the greatest number of Arab attacks on Israel came from the Egyptian-occupied Gaza Strip. Between 1954 and 1955, there were a total of 179 border incursions and some 429 armed clashes. Fifty-five Israelis were killed and 185 wounded.

In retaliation for the Egyptian attacks, the Israelis hit hard against the Egyptian military camp at Gaza. Forty Egyptians were killed in February 1955. Israeli forces suffered eight dead. A special session of the Security Council was requested by Egypt. The American representative declared that Israel's action was "indefensible from any standpoint," and the U.S. stood opposed to "any policy of reprisal or retaliation." Henry Cabot Lodge, Jr., the U.S. Ambassador to the U.N., went even further than that when he said that "whatever the provocation might have been in this case, there was no justification for the Israeli military action at Gaza." Israel had retaliated against an Egyptian military base because of the Egyptian attacks on Israeli civilians, but nothing was said about the Egyptian attacks, and Israel was unanimously censured by the Security Council on March 29, 1955.

While the Security Council debated and condemned the Israeli action without considering the Egyptian provocations, the Egyptians and the *Fedayeen* threw grenades and fired at a village called Patish, where a wedding was taking place. A woman was killed and eighteen guests were wounded. The Arab attacks continued, but the

U.N. and the world ignored Israel's sufferings, just as the world had ignored the Nazi extermination of six million European Jews a few years before.

THE BAGHDAD PACT

To counteract Soviet expansionist ambitions, the U.S. encouraged the development of a defense treaty which became known as the Baghdad Pact. This February 24, 1955 defense treaty between Iraq and Turkey was tied to an earlier treaty between Turkey and Pakistan. Iran and Britain joined, but the U.S. declined, even though Secretary of State Dulles had conceived the idea and the U.S. provided arms and money. Egyptian President Gamel Abdul Nasser was offended by the pact which he felt would deprive him of his position in the Arab world. He responded by seeking to overthrow the governments of Iraq and Jordan and building closer ties with the Kremlin. Nasser's arms deals with the Soviets in September 1955 were primarily a response to the Baghdad Pact, although some have claimed it was a reaction to an Israeli retaliatory raid into Gaza. As Abba Eban put it, Nasser could never forgive the West for "taking over the leadership of Arab international policy."[3]

Israel was alone. While the Arabs were being armed by the major powers, Israel had no steady source of supplies, nor did it have guarantees of security and integrity.

Added to Israel's increasing isolation, there were efforts to force the Jewish State to make territorial concessions to the Arabs. President Eisenhower wrote to Ben Gurion on April 10, 1956, and asked Israel to turn the other cheek: "I sincerely hope that in view of the terrible tragedy that general hostile actions will undoubtedly bring to this region, you will abstain, even under the pressure of extreme provocation, from any retaliatory acts which may result in very dangerous consequences."[4] Ben Gurion replied that if Eisenhower understood and appreciated the entire situation, he would never have restricted himself to "merely expressing the hope that we would abstain from military acts." Israel was grateful to the U.S. for its declaration that it would oppose any attack in this region, but such a statement did "not relieve our grave anxiety for Israel's security."[5]

A few days later, on the occasion of Israel's Independence Day celebration, Ben Gurion recalled how the world had failed to respond when Hitler's armies were hunting down and killing the people of

Israel. It seemed as if history was repeating itself in the 1950s. Egypt was arming itself and sending murder squads to kill Israelis while the world powers refused to sell arms to Israel, and they refused even to condemn the Arab atrocities. Ben Gurion wondered: "The conscience of the great powers failed when Hitler sent 6 million Jews of Europe to the Slaughter. Will that conscience fail again...?"[6]

An Israel self-defense action against Jordan almost brought a direct military confrontation between Israel and Britain. On October 10, 1956, Israeli forces retaliated for Jordanian incursions by decimating the Jordanian fort at Qahquilya. Jordan suffered many casualties and King Hussein demanded that Britain's Royal Air Force be brought in as per the Anglo-Jordanian Treaty. In his memoirs, Anthony Eden wrote that the R.A.F. was "on the point of going up," and the British Minister in Israel told Ben Gurion that if Israel attacked Jordan again, Britain would come to Jordan's assistance. But when he informed Ben Gurion that an Iraqi division would enter Jordan, the Israeli Prime Minister replied that Israel would feel free to take whatever action if felt necessary.

The Suez Canal should have been kept open to all nations according to the principles of international law, but Egypt closed it to Israel and to any ship that was either leaving or bound for an Israeli port. In response to Israel's complaint that Egypt was preventing it from using the Suez Canal, a resolution was introduced into the Security Council which noted "with grave concern" that Egypt had not complied with an earlier Council resolution (September 1, 1951) which had called on Egypt to "terminate the restrictions." But while the resolution received eight votes, it did not pass because the Soviet Union vetoed it.

The indifference of the world organization to Israel's plight continued as Egypt occupied the island of Tiran at the mouth of the Gulf of Eilat and then prevented Israeli shipping from using the port of Eilat. Israel protested, but the world remained indifferent to her plight. In September, 1954, the Israeli ship *Bat Galim* tried to pass through the Suez Canal in an effort to challenge Egypt's defiance of the U.N. resolution of 1951, and to encourage the U.N. to take further steps. Egypt seized the ship and its cargo, but released the ten crew members. Israel lodged a complaint before the Security Council on September 24, 1954, but the Council adjourned without passing any formal resolution or recommendation. There was no reference made to Israel's right of passage. The Council's presiding officer merely said that he hoped the affair would be settled by the Mixed Armistice Commission.

In addition to the *Fedayeen* attacks and the Egyptian closure of Suez and the Gulf of Eilat, there were other violations of the armistice agreements. In disregard of the armistice which provided for the orderly reactivation of the cultural and humanitarian institutions on Mount Scopus, free access to the holy places and cultural institutions, and the use of the cemetery on the Mount of Olives, the Jordanians kept Old Jerusalem closed to Israel.

SOVIET INFLUENCE

As Soviet influence in the Middle East increased, peace prospects decreased. Encouraging Arab nationalism from Iraq to Algeria, the Soviets gained influence throughout the Arab world. When the U.S. rejected an Egyptian request for $27 million in arms because it felt Egypt could not pay, the Egyptians turned to the Soviet Union and, in 1955, concluded an arms deal estimated at $200 million. The U.S. tried to prevent the Egyptians from consumating that deal by sending George Allen to Cairo, but he failed in his mission. On September 27, the arms agreement was publicly announced. During a foreign ministers' conference in Geneva, Secretary of State Dulles advised Soviet Foreign Minister Molotov that the arms deal with Egypt would make war in the Middle East more likely than ever.[7] But the Soviets were not about to change their minds.

In view of this growing threat to her security, Israel asked the U.S. for arms, but Eisenhower was opposed because he felt that "would only speed a Middle East arms race." Influenced by Eden, the President advised the Israelis to seek peace by ceding territory to Egypt.[8] Israeli Foreign Minister Sharett flew to Paris and later to Geneva to win help from the great powers, but all he got was a promise of a few planes from France. Israel was very much alone.

Dulles, in a further effort to forestall the Soviet arms deal, called for fixed permanent boundaries between Israel and her neighbors, and he suggested that Israel give up the Negev. At the same time, he spoke of a possible U.S. boundaries guarantee and the resettlement of Arab refugees where feasible. Eden went much further than that when he called for a compromise between the boundaries of the 1947 U.N. resolution and the 1949 armistice lines. He asked Israel to give up territories to both Egypt and Jordan. Ben Gurion rejected Eden's suggestions. They lacked "legal, moral and logical foundation." Sharett, in reply to Dulles, agreed to some mutual adjustments of the 1949 lines for security and communications purposes, but he refused to agree to the 1947 lines as a basis for negotiations. While Israel agreed to provide the Arab states with transit rights and port facilities, it would not agree to the creation of any extraterritorial corridor. Nor would Israel agree to unilateral concessions such as the surrender of Eilat or the Internationalization of Jerusalem.[9] The Anglo-American position of the 1950s was similar to what it had been towards free Europe in the 1930s. Unashamedly, they called for appeasement — Americans were prepared to reward Egypt, Syria. Lebanon and Jordan for their invasion of Israel. They suggested that aggressors and violators of international treaties should be rewarded. The Anglo-American position in the 1950s was similar to what it had been towards free Europe in the 1930s. But unlike the abdicators and appeasers of the 1930s, Israel refused to surrender its freedom. Except for France, whose empire was threatened by Algerian rebels supported by Soviet weapons received via Egypt, the Israelis had no friends. And France was a questionable ally.[10] France was willing to sell Egypt all the arms it wanted to destroy Israel, if only President Nasser would discontinue his support of the Algerian rebels. Nasser refused. Soviet Foreign Minister Shepilov went to Egypt while the Egyptians celebrated the British withdrawal from Suez with a display of Soviet arms. Shepilov was rumored to have offered Egypt an interest-free loan for a hydroelectric dam. To some, like Secretary of the Treasury George Humphrey, it seemed that Egypt was shopping around for the best offer.[11]

Nasser's recognition of Red China, his trade with Communist countries, and his interventionist activities in Yemen, Iraq, Jordan and Saudi Arabia, contributed to the decline of his popularity in the West. According to Raymond A. Hare, former head of the State Department's Middle East Division, "southern cotton growers were in fact opposed to the Aswan deal for fear it would increase competition with Egyptian cotton and their views were reflected in Congress, which had singled out the Aswan deal for criticism, and had demanded that there should be special consultation if it were included in the aid bill, which was then under consideration and having its usual difficulties."[12] Eisenhower concluded that America should not participate in the Aswan Dam project.[13]

Dulles revealed on July 10 that the loan to Egypt was "improbable." On the 13th, he informed the Egyptians that he could not deal with the dam question because he could not predict what action Congress might take, and that U.S. views had changed "on the merits of the matter."[14] On the 19th, Egypt's Ambassador asked Dulles not to say that America would withdraw the loan because he had a Soviet offer to finance the dam. Dulles shot back, "Well, as you have the money already, you don't need any from us! My offer is withdrawn!"[15]

When the U.S. announced its withdrawal from the project, Britain and the International Bank likewise withdrew. That brief exchange between Dulles and the Egyptian Ambassador represented the nadir point in the deteriorating relations between the U.S. and Egypt.

President Eisenhower felt that the cancellation of the loan was handled in a rather undiplomatic and abrupt manner, and he told Dulles how he felt. Dulles explained that there had been increasing Congressional opposition to the loan,[16] and he publicly announced the reasons for the United States' withdrawal from the Aswan Dam project:

> ...do nations which play both sides get better treatment than nations which are stalwart and work with us? That question was posed by the manner in which the Egyptians presented their final request to us, and Stalwart Allies were watching very carefully to see what the answer would be — stalwart allies which included some in the area.

After America said no, the Soviets did not appear anxious to build the Aswan Dam. On July 22, Foreign Minister Shepilov denied that he had made any firm commitment to build the dam. This may have encouraged President Nasser to denounce the U.S. before the entire world, and later proclaim the nationalization of the British-French owned Suez Canal Company with all its properties and assets in order to finance the construction of the Aswan Dam. He expected $100 million per year from the canal.

Threatened with extinction by the growing Soviet influence in the Middle East and Africa, the British and French prepared to destroy

Nasser, the Soviet Union's newly found ally. But President Eisenhower sought to discourage his NATO allies from intervening militarily against Egypt. For three months, he fathered various efforts to negotiate an agreement that would internationalize the canal while protecting "the sovereign rights of Egypt." The matter was even brought before the Security Council, but Soviet vetoes paralyzed that organization's effectiveness time and time again.

On July 27, 1956, Prime Minister Eden wrote the following appeal to President Eisenhower: "we cannot afford to allow Nasser to seize control of the Canal in this way....If we take a firm stand over this now, we shall have the support of all the maritime powers. If we do not, our influence and yours throughout the Middle East will...be finally destroyed....I am convinced that we must be ready, in the last resort, to use force to bring Nasser to his senses."[17]

Eisenhower continued to call for peaceful solutions. He was concerned with world public opinion and Soviet penetration among the developing areas. He was afraid that if his allies would intervene militarily in Egypt, then the Soviet Union's prestige among the developing nations would increase. He doubted whether such a move as Eden proposed would, in fact, bring stability to the area. He did not want the allies, and France in particular, to relate Nasser's actions to the Arab-Israeli difficulties. France had asked for U.S. approval to send additional jets to Israel, but Eisenhower was opposed. He thought it was a mistake "to link the two problems of the Canal and the Arab-Israeli borders."[18]

Deputy Under Secretary of State Robert Murphy reported on July 29, that for the time being, Britain and France would not use force, "pending the outcome of a conference of affected nations." The next day, Prime Minister Anthony Eden announced that Britain had cut off all aid to Egypt and that no arrangement for the Suez Canal would be acceptable if it left controls in the hands of any single state.

Throughout his communications with Britain and France, Eisenhower opposed the use of force. It would not work, was Eisenhower's argument. The history of India, Indochina and Algeria showed that occupying troops could not succeed unless they resorted to the brutalities of dictatorships and "we of the West, who believe in freedom and human dignity, could not descend to the use of Communist methods."[19]

During the morning of July 31, Dulles returned from a trip to

South America and brought Eisenhower a message he had just received from London that described Britain's firm decision to "break Nasser" at the earliest possible opportunity.[20] On that very day, Eisenhower sent Dulles flying to London with a message advising Anthony Eden that if England chose war, "the American reaction would be severe and that the great areas of the world would share that reaction."[21]

At his news conference in early September, Eisenhower declared that the U.S. was "...committed to a peaceful solution of this problem, and one that will insure to all nations the free use of the canal for the shipping of the world, whether in peace or in war, as contemplated by the 1888 convention." A week later, Eisenhower implied that America would not back Britain and France in case of war. America will "not go to war ever, while I am occupying my present post, unless the Congress is called into session, and Congress declares such a war." Dulles added that the U.S. would not "try to shoot its way through the Canal."[22]

THE SINAI CAMPAIGN

In the midst of the Suez debate, there were many confrontations between Israeli and Arab forces along the Israeli frontiers. Two Israeli military vehicles hit Egyptian mines on October 25, northwest of Kibbutz K'tziot in the Nitzana sector. Three soldiers were killed and twenty-seven wounded. On October 23, a three-way military pact was transacted by Egypt, Syria and Jordan, and Abdul Hakim Amer, the Egyptian Minister of War, was placed at its head. It was then that the commander of the Jordanian Legion, Ali Abu Nawar, proclaimed: "the time has come when the Arabs will be able to choose the time for an offensive to liquidate Israel." On October 27, as Israel mobilized, Eisenhower warned Ben Gurion not to start a war. In reply, Ben Gurion reminded Eisenhower that while Israel had supported his efforts to bring peace, Egypt had repeatedly called for Israel's destruction. He reviewed the military situation that Israel faced[23] and concluded by advising Eisenhower that Israel would not submit to subjugation at the hands of the Arabs. If Israel would not "take all possible measures to thwart the declared aim of the Arab rulers to destroy Israel" then it would not be "fulfilling its elementary responsibilities."[24]

Ben Gurion anticipated trouble from many countries, but mainly

from the U.S. On October 28, as he reviewed the need to destroy
Fedayeen bases, and to secure unhampered passage through the
Straits of Tiran, he told his cabinet that he did not expect Jordan and
Syria would intervene to help Egypt. But in any case, Israeli forces
would be placed on full alert along the eastern flank. India, Africa
and the Soviet Union might intervene against Israel, but what
worried Ben Gurion most was the United States. The Soviets would
have to use military force to impose their will, but the U.S. would not
have to send one boy to the Middle East in order to harm Israel.

The United States had economic and other weapons with which to
intimidate Israel. But whatever the cost, Israel would have to take
measures to defend itself.[25] If Israel failed to safeguard its existence,
no one else would.

Hostilities began on October 29. Israel penetrated Sinai and Gaza,
and within a matter of one hundred hours, defeated the Egyptian
Army.[26] On October 30, as per an Israeli-British-French understanding,[27] Britain and France informed the Security Council that
they had called on the belligerents to withdraw their forces to a
distance of ten miles from Suez. If the combatants would not meet
those conditions within twelve hours, Britain and France would
intervene to safeguard the canal and restore peace. Israel agreed to
the cease-fire, but Egypt refused and Anglo-French forces attacked
Egyptian military installations in the Suez Canal area. In turn, Egypt
sank ships in the canal and closed it to all, and when British and
French troops landed in the Port Said area on November 5, the Soviet
Union threatened to send volunteers against Israel, and missiles
against Britain and France. When Soviet Premier Bulganin proposed
that America join him against the British, French and Israelis, Eisenhower responded by calling the Soviet suggestion "unthinkable"
and he placed U.S. forces on alert. Eisenhower warned Bulganin
that any entry of new troops into the Middle East would force U.N.
members to take effective counter-measures.

Eisenhower had taken the initiative to condemn Israel, Britain and
France. On the day the war began, he informed the Security Council
that Israeli forces had invaded Sinai in violation of the armistice
agreement, and he requested an immediate meeting to consider the
"Palestine question: steps for the immediate cessation of military
action of Israel in Egypt." The Soviet Ambassador "warmly welcomed" the Eisenhower position. Perhaps U.S. and Soviet spokes-

men differed in tone, but the substance of their position was the same. Disregarding Egyptian violations, the United States charged the State of Israel with violating the armistice, called on Israel to withdraw, and demanded that all U.N. members "refrain from giving any military, economic or financial assistance to Israel as long as it had not complied with the resolution." The Council considered the question from October 30 to November 1, but it could not act because of British and French vetoes. The U.S. then engineered an emergency session of the General Assembly to remedy the situation.

That General Assembly adopted a resolution on November 2 which called for a cease-fire and the reopening of the Suez Canal.[28] Furthermore, the General Assembly urged the parties of the Armistice Agreements of 1949 to promptly "withdraw all forces behind armistice lines...desist from raids across the armistice lines to neighboring territory, and...observe scrupulously the provisions of the Armistice Agreements...." A day later, Henry Cabot Lodge, Jr., expressed the United States' regret that the U.N. resolution had not been complied with, but he added that America was convinced that the problems which had given rise to the situation could and had to be "solved by peaceful and just means." This time, the Americans said that while it was the duty of the U.N. to see to it that a cease-fire takes place, they believed "the problems and conditions" which had created the situation should not be disregarded, and Lodge introduced resolutions to help solve those problems.

The first resolution concerned "Palestine" and suggested the creation of a five-member committee which was to prepare recommendations for the General Assembly after having consulted the interested parties. The second resolution concerned Suez and adhered to the draft resolution of October 12, 1956, which provided for a three-member committee with responsibilities to take measures necesary for the immediate reopening of the canal, to draw up a plan in consultation with the three nations most directly concerned for the purpose of operating and maintaining the canal, and to put such a plan into effect. This committee was to report to the General Assembly and the Security Council.

On November 5, the U.S. supported a Canadian resolution which authorized the Secretary General to establish a U.N. Emergency Force to supervise the cessation of hostilities. Although Eisenhower expressed America's readiness to assist the U.N. force with supplies and transportation, the U.S. would not contribute troops.

But despite Eisenhower's valiant efforts at impartiality, the Arab states remained suspicious of American intentions. They felt that Washington had sought a settlement favorable to the Western powers and to Israel. And their suspicions seemed to have been confirmed when the U.S. rejected a Soviet suggestion that American and Soviet forces unite to halt hostilities.

SOVIET AND AMERICAN THREATS

Both American and Soviet leaders threatened Israel. On November 5, 1956, Premier Nikolai A. Bulganin wrote Premier Ben Gurion that Israel was acting according to instructions from others and that it was "toying with the fate of peace, with the fate of its own people, in a criminal and irresponsible manner." He warned that its very "existence" was in "jeopardy." Two days later, President Eisenhower wrote Ben Gurion of his "deep concern" with Israel's unwillingness to withdraw. He urged immediate compliance with the U.N. General Assembly resolution.

Herbert Hoover, Jr., on behalf of Secretary Dulles, who was hospitalized, summoned Israeli Ambassador Reuven Shiloah and presented him with an oral supplement to the Eisenhower letter of November 7. Again, Israel was told that its actions had threatened the peace since the Soviets were creating a menacing and disastrous situation and that Israel would be the first to perish since it refused to withdraw as the U.N. commanded. He concluded that the Israeli position would result in the discontinuance of all U.S. assistance (government and private), U.N. sanctions and expulsion from the U.N. That was the communication from a diplomat whose nation was presumably on good terms with Israel.[29]

The Secretary General reported on November 7 that a cease-fire had been achieved, but peace was still a distant prospect. Foreign troops were still in Egypt and the exact role of the U.N. troops was undefined.

By November 7, Israel was threatened with Soviet military intervention and American economic sanctions, as well as expulsion from the U.N. Ben Gurion had declared that Israel would not permit foreign troops to set foot on any of the occupied areas, but the combined Soviet-American pressure was too much for the Israeli leadership, and Ben Gurion backed down. Israel made its withdrawal from Sharm El-Sheik and Gaza conditional on the deployment of U.N.E.F. in those areas, and ultimately, the U.S. and the U.N. accepted those Israeli conditions.

By December 3, Britain and France agreed to "complete withdrawal" and by December 22, they completed that withdrawal. Golda Meir met with Secretary Dulles toward the end of December and assured him that Israel wanted to live on good terms with the U.S. and the U.N. But again, Meir asked the U.S. to support freedom of passage through the Straits of Tiran, and the non-return of the Gaza Strip to Egypt. She also asked Dulles to convince Dag Hammarskjold to postpone any change in Sinai and Gaza until a settlement could be reached.

Dulles supported freedom of navigation through the Straits, and he admitted that Gaza was never Egyptian; but he reminded Golda Meir that the armistice agreement had not made it Israeli territory either. So he advised her to work things out through the U.N.

Israel agreed to evacuate Sinai by January 22, but she still refused to evacuate Sharm El-Sheik, and she asked that further debate on that question be postponed until some concrete guarantees had been worked out for freedom of navigation through the Straits. But the U.N. did not listen. On February 2, the General Assembly by a vote of 74 to 2, called for Israeli withdrawal from both Gaza and Sharm El-Sheik with the provision that U.N.E.F. would be placed there. This was followed by further American pressures on Israel.

On February 4, Eisenhower warned that Israel's disregard of international opinion would "almost certainly lead to further U.N. action which will seriously damage relations between Israel and U.N. members, including the U.S."[30] A day later, he declared that the U.S. was seriously considering the application of economic sanctions against Israel. But Israel would not withdraw from Sharm El-Sheik or the Gaza Strip unless it was guaranteed freedom of passage through the Gulf of Eilat, and unless U.N. troops were placed in the Gaza Strip to help prevent *Fedayeen* attacks on Israel. Eisenhower proclaimed that unless Israel would withdraw "forthwith" he could not "predict the consequences." As the U.S. indicated its willingness to support sanctions, Ben Gurion responded that Israel would not accept the double standard pursued by the U.N.: "Israel though small is entitled to security, freedom and equal rights in the family of nations. Like any other independent nation, Israel is free as of right and our people are determined to defend their independence."

On February 11, the U.S. promised Israel that U.N. troops would be placed in Gaza and there would be freedom of passage through the Straits if Israel withdrew. But the February 11 promise was not enough, since it required withdrawal from Gaza and Sharm El-Sheik in advance of the settlement. Israel was concerned lest the U.N.E.F. might be precipitately withdrawn, passage through the Gulf of Eilat obstructed and the fighting renewed.

Israelis were not the only ones disappointed with Eisenhower's approach. Many members of Congress were likewise disappointed. Republican Senator William Knowland of California told Eisenhower that if sanctions were imposed, they had first to be applied against the Soviet Union for its invasion of Hungary. Senate Majority Leader Lyndon B. Johnson opposed the Eisenhower approach and called for guarantees to protect Israel against Egyptian incursions and threats in the Gulf of Eilat. The Senate Democratic Policy Committee unanimously approved Johnson's statement and called on Eisenhower to resist any U.N. effort to impose sanctions against Israel. Johnson's letter to Eisenhower of February 19, 1957, stated that the U.N. could not "apply one rule for the strong and another for the weak...." There had been no U.N. sanctions imposed on the U.S.S.R. for its invasion of Hungary. Israel "complied with the directives of the U.N. Russia has not even pretended to be polite...."

Eisenhower insisted things had to go his way, and he said so before a nationwide television broadcast:

> I do not believe that Israel's default should be ignored because the U.N. has not been able to effectively carry out its resolutions condemning the Soviet Union for its armed suppression of the people of Hungary. Perhaps this is a case where the proverb applies that two wrongs do not make a right.
>
> The present moment is a grave one, but we are hopeful that reason and right will prevail. Since the events of last October - November, solid progress has been made, in conformity with the Charter of the U.N. There is a cease-fire, the forces of Britain and France have been withdrawn, and the clearing of the Canal nears completion. When Israel completes its withdrawal, it will have removed a definite block to further progress.

After negotiations with the Great Powers, Secretary General Hammarskjold issued a memorandum on February 26, assuring Israel that any proposal for the withdrawal of U.N.E.F. would first have to be submitted to the Advisory Committee which represented the General Assembly. As the General Assembly debate began, Foreign Minister Meir announced on March 1 that Israel had agreed to "full and complete withdrawal" on the basis of the Secretary General's report of February 26. Israel would withdraw on condition that U.N.E.F. would be placed in Gaza, and the U.N. would be responsible for the area until a peace settlement or a definitive agreement on the future of Gaza would be reached. Moreover, Israel warned that it would reserve its freedom of action if threatened by a return to October 1956 conditions. As for the Gulf of Eilat and the Straits, Meir declared Israel's readiness to withdraw from Sharm El-Sheik "in the confidence that there will be continued freedom of navigation for international and Israeli shipping in the Gulf and the Straits of Tiran." Israel would regard any interference with her rights of passage as an "attack entitling her to exercise her inherent right of self-defense...."[31]

Meir's March 1 speech had been "drafted in consultation with the United States" and with the endorsement of the "French, British and all the major maritime nations." The U.S. and France had provided Israel with what she had requested. Eban recalled that the U.S. "in clear terms and France, in even more vigorous language, stated they would support Israel as she exercised her right of self-defense against any renewal of the blockade in the Straits of Tiran or any resumption of *fedayeen* raids from Gaza." But when Lodge addressed the General Assembly that day, he omitted the understanding on Gaza. So Israel delayed her withdrawal until the Gaza matter was cleared up. Only after Eisenhower reassured Ben Gurion that he supported Meir's statement was Israel prepared to withdraw.[32]

Ben Gurion still believed that Israel should not have withdrawn. In a letter to Eisenhower, he said that the only reason Israel did withdraw was because of the President's March 2 letter which had reassured Israel that it "would have no cause to regret" and that its "hopes and expectations" would "not prove groundless." There were careful and detailed agreements to ensure that Eisenhower's commitments to Israel would manifest themselves concretely. As agreed, a ship flying the U.S. flag passed through the Straits of

Tiran. The Egyptians were not stopped, however, when they sent in their personnel back to Gaza in violation of the understandings. Despite all the fine documents and agreements, Israel was very much alone. Within a few short years, Israel's future was again threatened by the Arabs and their Soviet friends and she found that the 1957 commitments of the U.S., Western Europe, and the U.N. could not help save her.

As a result of Eisenhower's 1956 diplomacy, Soviet influence greatly increased while Western influence declined in the Middle East and throughout the underdeveloped world. The West, especially the U.S., was singled out as interventionist and imperialist, while the Soviet Union and Egypt were considered emancipators. Suez remained in Egyptian hands, and after continued Soviet and Egyptian support of the Algerian rebels, France was forced to withdraw from Algeria in 1958. The Israeli victory of 1956 had enabled the Jewish State to survive, but because of Great Power intervention, there was still no peace in the Middle East, and by 1967, Israel's fears regarding the worthlessness of the February 1957 guarantees would be substantiated. Furthermore, the U.S. attempt to restore the moral position and influence of the West in Asia and Africa was a blow to NATO from which it would never recover. Charles de Gaulle would drive NATO out of France.

Once more, there had been lots of diplomacy but little rescue. Major Power intervention only resulted in greater confusion. If they had kept clear, the nations of the Middle East might have come to some mutual understanding. Their intervention not only prevented a settlement, but it ultimately forced the major powers to use greater force in the Middle East in order to uphold their positions. The Soviets would pour greater quantities of military hardware into Egypt, Syria and Iraq, while Eisenhower would come forward with a proclamation against further Communist intervention which he would have to back up with American troops in Lebanon.

As in 1948-49, so in 1956, Israel had been very much alone. If not for her ability to defend herself, Israel would have been eliminated. Instead of helping her in 1956-57, the U.N. and the U.S. in particular, put Israel in greater danger by encouraging the Soviet cancer in Egypt to grow. Israel's isolation would be evident once again in 1967, and again in 1973, when the Arabs and Soviets would again conspire to destroy the Jewish State.

1 During this time, the U.S. discontinued its assistance to the development project at *Bnot Ya'akov*. The aid to the water project was not renewed until a great deal of public pressure was exerted in the U.S.

2 Abba Eban, *My Country* (New York, 1972) 122-23.

3 *Ibid*. 125-36; Arie Bober, ed. *The Other Israel* (New York, 1972); Kenneth Love, *Suez, Twice Fought War* (New York, 1969).

4 Ben Gurion, *Israel: A Personal History* (New York, 1972) 474-76, Hereafter cited as Ben Gurion, *Personal History*.

5 *Ibid*.

6 *Ibid*.

7 Hugh Thomas, *Suez* (New York, 1967) 15-16. Hereafter cited as Thomas, *Suez*.

8 Dwight D. Eisenhower, *Waging Peace* (New York, 1965) 25. Hereafter cited as Eisenhower, *Waging Peace*.

9 Eban, *My Country*, 129-130.

10 During World War II, when Syria was under Vichy rule, the Jews of Erez Israel helped Charles de Gaulle maintain contact with the French underground in Syria and Lebanon. Both the French High Command and the people of France appreciated the heroism of the Haganah before the State of Israel was proclaimed, but it took France several months after Israel's declaration of independence to extend recognition.

When Guy Mollet came to power in early 1956, the deal to supply Israel with arms was undertaken without the knowledge of the French Foreign Ministry, but with Foreign Minister Christian Pineau's personal and active participation. The French equipment helped rescue Israel's "military strength" according to Abba Eban. By the time Nasser announced his nationalization, the idea that France might help Israel to resist Egyptian pressure was already familiar to some parts of both the Israeli and French governments.

See Eban *My Country*, 132-33.

On June 20, 1956, two destroyers arrived in Israel. One was the *Eilat* and the other was the *Yafo*. They were brought in by an Israeli crew that had spent several months training with the British Navy. From July to September 1956, the balance of arms was improved with the arrival of tanks, guns, planes and ammunition from France. Without this equipment, Israel would have been at the mercy of the Arab arsenals which had been filled mainly by the Soviet Union and the United States.

11 Thomas, *Suez*, 17.

12 Interview with Raymond A. Hare, January 27, 1970.

13 In its deliberations on the Aswan Dam funds, the Senate Appropriateions Committee declared that money for the Aswan Dam could not be used for that project "without prior approval of the Committee of Appropriations." Eisenhower refused to accept that codicil because it would have cut into the President's constitutional powers. Eisenhower, *Waging Peace*, 32.

14 *Ibid*.

15 Herman Finer, *Dulles Over Suez, The Theory and Practice of His Diplomacy*, (Chicago, 1964), 47-48.

16 *Ibid*., 33.

17 Anthony Eden, *Full Circle,* 428.

18 Eisenhower, *Waging Peace,* 36-38.

19 *Ibid.,* 40.

20 *Ibid.*

21 *Ibid.,* 41, 664-665.

22 Eban, *My Country,* 131-32.
The American statements served to deprive Australia's Prime Minister Robert Menzies of his bargaining position while he was talking with Egyptians on behalf of the London Conference of Canal Users. Nasser rejected a proposed compromise that would have provided for international supervision of Suez while the Canal and its company would remain in Egyptian hands. The rift between the U.S. and her allies widened.

23 The Arabs were fully equipped and they once again made ready to destroy Israel. In jet planes alone, Egypt outnumbered Israel 305 to 79.

24 Ben Gurion, *Personal History,* 503-504.

25 *Ibid.,* 504-505.

26 The casualty figures differ from source to source. Ben Gurion reports that 171 Israelis were killed and one pilot wounded and taken prisoner. Abba Eban tells us that 180 were killed and four taken prisoner. The Egyptians lost over 1,000 killed and 6,000 taken prisoner.

27 Michael Bar Zohar sums up the history of the development that resulted in the semi-alliance between Israel, France and Great Britain. See *Ben Gurion, The Armed Prophet* (New Jersey, 1966).

28 The five who opposed were Australia, Britain, France, Israel and New Zealand. In addition, there were six abstentions.

29 Ben Gurion, *Personal History,* 514.

30 *Ibid.,* 524-25.

31 Eban, *My Country,* 148-49.

32 Ben Gurion, *Personal History,* 532-33.

Chapter VI

Six Days In June

In the various diplomatic meeting places, the debate involving Israel and the Arabs continued. Most, if not all, were disputatious and inconclusive. When the U.N. had an opportunity to improve matters, and to rise above pedestrian disputations, it failed to take action. In December 1961, the General Assembly failed to approve a resolution offered by sixteen delegations which called on the Arabs and Israelis to undertake "direct negotiations with a view to finding a solution acceptable to all the parties concerned, for all the questions in dispute between them." Israel welcomed the resolution, the Arabs rejected it, and the General Assembly's Special Political Committee defeated it by a vote of 44 to 34 with 20 abstentions and 6 absent.

The Arab attacks continued. By 1966, conditions had become unbearable. Syrian guns unremittingly bombarded Israel's northern settlements. In early October 1966, Syrian based terrorists raided Israeli cities and placed explosives in residential areas. Throughout this period of repeated provocations, the Israelis were pressured by Washington not to retaliate, but to bring it all before the U.N. Israel yielded and found the U.S., Japan, Britain, China, Argentina, the Netherlands and New Zealand praising Israel for its good behavior, but the Soviet Union, Bulgaria, Jordan and Mali continued to condemn Israel as the aggressor, while they exonerated Syria of all guilt. The debate dragged on for weeks. The end result was a meaningless and empty resolution which invited Syria "to strengthen its measures for preventing incidents that constitute a violation of the general Armistice Agreement." Israel was asked to "cooperate

fully with the Israel-Syria Mixed Armistice Commission." Ten of
the Security Council members voted for the tepid resolution. Four
rejected it, and the Soviet Union was one of the four. Even that
meaningless resolution failed to win approval. Nikolai T. Federenko, the bow-tied ex-school teacher representing the Soviets, explained his veto by complaining that the resolution had been "one-
sided" and that it accused Syria of negligence.

United Nations inaction encouraged the Arabs to commit further
war acts against Israel. Syria signed a defense agreement with Egypt
and a week later, on November 12, an Israeli command car was
blown up by a mine in the Hebron Hills region. Three soldiers were
killed and six wounded.

When on November 13, Israeli forces hit the Jordanian village of
Es Samu as a warning to Jordan against aiding saboteurs and terrorists, Jordan called on the Security Council to impose sanctions
against Israel. During the debate, the Western representatives com-
peted with African and Soviet representatives in their condemnation
of Israel, and a resolution was passed which censured Israel without
even mentioning the terrorist provocations.

And so it was year, after year, after year.

From 1956 to 1967, Israel learned that it could not expect justice
or protection from the U.N. or any of its members.

THE NORTH IN 1967

Israelis in the Galilee were subjected to Syrian machine guns,
artillery and aircraft. In response to those provocations, Israel sent
up its planes to silence the enemy. On April 7, 1967, Israeli pilots
shot down six Syrian MIGs. Egypt, spurred by the Soviet Union,
sent political and military missions to Syria to establish a closer war
alignment.

As the terrorist activities from Syria increased, the Soviet Union
claimed that the terrorists were agents of American oil interests and
that the Central Intelligence Agency was seeking to provoke Israeli
retaliation and weaken the Syrian regime. Israel asked the Soviet
Union to intervene in Syria and attempt to halt the terrorism, but
instead of calming the situation, the Soviets encouraged Egypt to
fight Israel so as to remove the so-called burden from Syria. Anwar
Sadat, President of the National Council, and head of the Egyptian
parliamentary delegation to Moscow, was told by Soviet officials to

"expect an Israeli invasion." The Egyptians seemed to have accepted the Soviet line, and President Nasser imposed a blockade of the Straits of Tiran on May 22.[1]

Prime Minister Eshkol invited the Soviet Ambassador to visit the allegedly mobilized areas, but the Soviets declined that invitation. The U.N. investigated the Soviet charges, and Secretary General U Thant publicly declared that there were no exceptional troop concentrations in the area. The U.S. likewise informed the Soviets that Israel was not massing its troops on the Syrian frontiers, and when President Johnson learned that Moscow had promised unlimited support to the Syrians, he asked them if this were so. The Soviets denied all knowledge of such a pledge.[2]

Nasser mobilized his troops on May 14, 1967, and two days later, when he asked the U.N. to withdraw its troops from Sinai, Secretary General U Thant complied. President Johnson was apparently shocked, and from what he wrote in his memoirs, it appeared as if the Egyptians had not expected U Thant to react that way. U Thant did not present the matter before the Security Council, or the General Assembly, nor did he harken to Israel's advice that U.N.E.F. withdrawal "should not be achieved by a unilateral UAR (United Arab Republic; Syria & Egypt) request alone." The Israeli government urged him "to avoid condoning any changes in the *status quo* pending the fullest and broadest international consultations." U Thant disregarded the Israeli request and the region moved closer to war.[3]

Johnson cabled Eshkol on May 17 that he could not "accept any responsibilities on behalf of the U.S. for situations which arise as the result of actions on which we are not consulted." President Johnson wrote Premier Kosygin that the U.S. and the Soviet Union should work together "in the cause of moderation...." He also sent Nasser a message reassuring him of American friendship and understanding, and he urged him to avoid war. The President suggested that he might send Vice President Humphrey to help find a solution to the old problems there. But, as Johnson sent his cables and letters, Nasser announced the closure of the Gulf of Eilat to Israeli shipping. Said Nasser: "The Jews have threatened war, and we say to them: Come and get it, Egypt is ready!"[4]

U.N.E.F. withdrawal from Sinai, and the Egyptian seizure of the Gulf of Eilat, smashed the 1957 settlement. Israel now had to attend to its self-defense or face further losses. On March 1, 1957, Ambassador Lodge had affirmed a U.S.-Israeli agreement that Israeli withdrawal from Sinai was tied to free passage through the Gulf of Eilat and that any interference would enable Israel to undertake self-defense measures. One week earlier, Dulles had informed President Eisenhower in a memo "that Israel has been assured that a purpose of UNEF would be to restrain the exercise of belligerent rights which would prevent passage through the Straits of Tiran." President Eisenhower was called upon to clarify its meaning. When Eisenhower confirmed that Israel's right of access through the Gulf of Eilat was part of the American commitment, Johnson declared on May 23, 1967, that the Egyptian blockade was "illegal" and that it was "potentially disastrous to the cause of peace." He also condemned the mobilization of forces, called for peace, and reiterated American support for the political independence and territorial integrity of all nations in that region.

Canada and Denmark called for a Security Council meeting which convened at 10:30 a.m. on May 24, but the Soviet representative, Nikolai T. Federenko, "did not see sufficient grounds for such a hasty convening of the Security Council." The Soviet Union disputed the necessity for calling the Council, and Egypt declared that it was going to wipe Israel off the map.

The Soviet Union and its friends preferred to await the return of U Thant from his Middle Eastern journey. But the United States insisted on opening discussions, and so did Japan, Canada, Denmark and Great Britain. The Council members passed a resolution supporting U Thant's pacification efforts and they requested the concerned parties to refrain from taking any steps that might worsen the situation. It reconvened on May 29 to hear that U Thant had returned empty-handed. Egypt declared that "a state of war" existed in the Middle East, and the Soviets complained that Israel was aggravating the situation.

The world watched the endless debate of the highly trained and educated double-talking U.N. ambassadors. Each sovereign state continued to conduct itself according to its own selfish interests.

Prime Minister Eshkol sent Foreign Minister Eban to find help from abroad. On his way to Washington, Eban visited French and British leaders. President de Gaulle admired Eban's French and advised Israel not to fire the first shot. When Eban reminded de Gaulle that French commitments to aid Israel if the Straits of Tiran would be blockaded "had been more dramatic and unequivocal than any other," the French leader maintained that the "guarantees were not absolute and the situation had evolved." France wanted Israel to wait for a Big Four (U.S., French, British and Soviet) effort to break the blockade. When Eban saw Britain's Prime Minister Wilson, he heard of his determination to see the Straits open, but that determination was based upon what the United States and others might be ready to do.[5]

A few days later, the Israelis saw President Johnson. Eban informed the President that Israeli intelligence reports indicated Egypt was preparing for an all-out attack against Israel. L.B.J. replied that U.S. intelligence indicated that Nasser had neither the intention nor the strength to attack Israel, and if Egypt tried to attack, Israel would "whip the hell out of them."[6]

When Eban asked what the U.S. might do to keep the Gulf of Eilat open, President Johnson replied that he had stated his position on May 23, and that he was working on how to assure freedom of access. "You can assure the Israeli Cabinet," said President Johnson, "we will pursue vigorously any and all possible measures to keep the straits open." But he insisted that matters had first to be worked out through the U.N. Johnson believed he could gather an international armada in support of free access, but he wanted to make sure that he had the support of Congress. Because of the Viet Nam embroilments, L.B.J. seemed unwilling to make a move without the backing of Congress. "I am fully aware of what three past Presidents have said, but that is not worth five cents," said L.B.J., "if the people and the Congress do not support the President."[7] He then promised that Israel would not be "alone" unless it decided to go it alone.

But could Israel afford to wait and see? Israel, insisted Eban, was faced with a "clear cut choice, surrender or fight" and the people of Israel were "unanimous not to surrender."[8]

Johnson insisted that if Israel wanted "some proximity" with the U.S. in the future, it would have to "invest some time." He needed two weeks to organize that international flotilla. "I am neither weak nor scared," concluded Johnson, "I've got to face out this thing."[9]

At half past two in the morning of May 27, Levi Eshkol was awakened by Soviet Ambassador Dimitri Chuvakin who insisted on an interview. Chuvakin sumbitted a note which accused the Israelis of collaboration with "imperialist powers" against Syria and Egypt and it warned Israel to "...avoid a clash of arms that will have serious consequences for the cause of peace and international security." Eshkol studied the note carefully, tried to explain the Israeli position, but his words fell on deaf ears. Chuvakin was sent to deliver advice, not to accept proposals.[10]

A few hours before this, Nasser had received President Johnson's cable asking Egypt not to engage in combat. While the Soviet Ambassador to Egypt went to see President Nasser and ask him "not to undertake any military action," the Soviets wrote President Johnson, defending the Egyptian moves while attacking the Israelis. Again, the Soviets warned that the U.S. should "take all measures possible to avoid a military conflict...." Telegrams and ambassadors were flying fast.

Just when Eshkol received the Soviet note accusing Israel of collaboration with so-called imperialist powers against Syria and Egypt, he received a note from President Johnson advising him not to take military action. L.B.J. quoted Kosygin, who threatened Soviet intervention if the Arabs were attacked.[11]

Israel harkened to L.B.J.'s appeals for restraint, but the Israelis were unsure of his ability to remove the danger. The danger increased on May 30, when King Hussein of Jordan, a long time rival of Nasser's, signed a pact declaring that "the armies of Egypt, Jordan, Syria and Lebanon are stationed on the borders of Israel. Behind them stand the armies of Iraq, Algeria, Kuwait, Sudan and the whole Arab nation.... The hour of decision has arrived." By June 4, Iraq formally joined the Egyptian-Jordanian pact. Confronted with all this, Israel's patience came to an end.

On May 31, Premier Eshkol appointed Moshe Dayan, Chief of Staff for the Israeli forces during the 1956 war, as his Minister of Defense. Almost as if to reassure Lyndon Johnson, who was deeply committed and preoccupied with Viet Nam, the new Defense Minister told the world on June 5 that his country could win the war without the aid of foreign troops, and he did not want "anyone else to fight for us...."

Johnson sought Security Council endorsement of an appeal U Thant had made to keep the peace, but because France abstained, the U.S. was unable to muster the required nine votes for passage. But he also failed to muster international support for a maritime power declaration that the Gulf of Eilat was an international waterway. After great effort, he had gathered only eight states to back a declaration supporting innocent passage. Those included: Israel, U.S., Britain, Netherlands, Australia, Iceland, Belgium and New Zealand. West Germany, Argentina, Portugal, Canada and Panama were considering the matter.

Rusk cabled Arab leaders urging them to seek solutions to prevent war. He advised them that it would "do no good to ask Israel simply to accept the present *status quo* in the Strait," because Israel will fight and we cannot restrain her, "we cannot abandon, in principle, the right of Israeli flag ships to transit the Strait."[12]

Eban reported home that President Johnson would break the blockade within two weeks. Despite intelligence reports that Moscow would not fight, Johnson's main concern was Congress' extreme sensitivity to unilateral Presidential commitments of troops. After hearing Eban's report, the Israeli Cabinet decided to postpone military action. On May 30, Eshkol assured Johnson that Eban's conversation with the President had "an important influence on our decision to await developments for a further limited period." It was "crucial that the international naval escort should move through the Straits of Tiran within a week or two."

When Rusk told Johnson that Congress preferred a multinational approach rather than unilateral U.S. intervention, Johnson said that he wanted to work through the U.N., but he did not have much faith in that body. "I've never relied on it to save me when I'm going down for the third time." He believed he had about two weeks to make diplomacy work. Israeli generals had informed Prime Minister Eshkol that every day of inaction would cost Israel over two hundred military deaths and that the partial mobilization was costing between $15 and $20 million per day in lost crops and economic production.

On June 2, Israeli Ambassador Avraham Harmon informed Dean Rusk that the test of the Tiran Straits would be made "during the next week." Robert Anderson, former Secretary of the Treasury under Eisenhower, was in Egypt and met with Nasser on May 31. He arranged for the U.A.R. Vice President to meet with President Johnson on June 7. Israel became concerned lest the Arabs and Americans would make some sort of deal against Israel.

THE SIX DAY WAR

Fighting broke out on June 5 along Israel's southern frontier. As Egyptian planes were sighted on radar, Israeli aircraft went up and, within a few short hours, the Israeli Air Force gained domination of the air by knocking out the Soviet-built Egyptian aircraft. Egyptian ground forces in Gaza bombarded Israeli settlements and Israeli armoured units responded fully. After finishing the Egyptians, Israel met and defeated the Jordanians, Iraqi and eventaully Syrian forces.[13]

One of the most dramatic battles of the war ended shortly after 10 a.m. on June 7 when Israeli troops gained control of the Old City of Jerusalem and restored the city's unity for the first time since 1948. It had taken the Israeli troops some forty-seven hours to win control of the Jerusalem area. The fighting there ended when an Israeli column penetrated through St. Stephen's Gate and swept through the ancient city. Israeli troops, in full battle dress, prayed at the Western Wall within minutes of recapturing the greatest shrine of Judaism. It was a rare moment in history.

Israel had achieved all its military objectives at a cost of 679 dead and 2,563 wounded, compared to 171 dead in the 1956 Suez campaign. Israeli forces held the entire Sinai up to the East Bank of Suez, Gaza, the West Bank of the Jordan River, and the Golan Heights. They had destroyed the combined armed forces of Egypt, Jordan and Syria. On June 9, General Dwight D. Eisenhower compared the Israeli military forces to "the patriots' army who stuck it out through the winter at Valley Forge." He felt that the Israeli troops had the same dedication as George Washington's troops.[14]

At 4:30 a.m., President Johnson was told that the war was on. He instructed Secretary of State Dean Rusk to cable the Soviets that the U.S. wanted the Security Council to bring an end to the fighting. Johnson did not get much sleep.

4:30 a.m. - Call from Rostow
5:09 a.m. - Call from Rusk
6:15 a.m. - Call from Christian
6:40 a.m. - Breakfast
6:49 a.m. - Call from Rostow
6:55 a.m. - Call from Rostow
7:50 a.m. - Call from Goldberg
7:57 a.m. - Call from McNamara.[15]

At 7:57 a.m., Secretary of Defense Robert McNamara informed L.B.J. that there was a message on the hot line from Chairman Kosygin. The President then joined Rusk, McNamara and Walt Rostow in the White House Situation Room to receive the message. Kosygin said that he planned to work for a cease-fire and he hoped the U.S. would exert its influence over Israel. The President replied that the U.S. would exert its influence over Israel to bring an end to the fighting and he publicly asked "all parties to support the Security Council in bringing about an immediate cease-fire." Later in the day, at 7 p.m., Kosygin was on the hot line again. this time he issued an ultimatum that if Israel did not withdraw, the Soviet Union would use appropriate means to end "Israeli aggression." L.B.J. responded by sending the U.S. Sixth Fleet closer to the fighting zone and he advised Kosygin of America's commitment to Israeli independence. He concluded by suggesting that the Soviet Union and the United States should act constructively.[16]

In discussion with various interested parties, the U.S. declared that it was prepared to support an immediate cease-fire, but that a withdrawal of Israeli forces had to be accompanied by a commitment of all parties in the area to refrain from "acts of force regardless of their nature."

Arthur Goldberg, the U.S. Ambassador to the U.N., met with Egypt's Ambassador to the U.N. and urged him to accept a mutual withdrawal from Sinai. But the Egyptians still hoped to obtain a cease-fire and a withdrawal of Israeli forces without any Egyptian concessions. They refused to go along with the U.S. suggestions, and they accused the U.S. of aggression. In turn, State Department spokesman Robert J. McClosky asserted that the U.S. would be neutral in thought as well as in action. While Israel fought for its very life, some Department of State officials unearthed an old Wilsonian cliche, that had been inappropriate even in 1914, to describe U.S. policy in 1967. This, at a time when Johnson was trying to convince the Soviet Union that the United States would not stand by during Soviet intervention. According to President Johnson's memoirs, McClosky's statement may have been "designed to reassure the Arabs that we were not engaged in the hostilities...."[17]

There was angry public reaction to McClosky's statement. Senator Dirksen, Republican from Illinois, asserted that the United States should "not be a party to negotiating away any of those rights that the Israelis may establish through their own military efforts.'' Senator Joseph Clark, Democrat from Pennsylvania, said that "morally as well as legally, we are an ally of Israel. We are not neutral.'' Senator Robert F. Kennedy, Democrat of New York, called for a "permanent and enforceable settlement of all out-standing issues,'' and he asked for guarantees of Israeli security from invasion and the right to pass through the Gulf of Eilat and the Suez Canal. In response to all this, the President's Press Secretary explained that McClosky "did not mean that the U.S. (was) neutral and indifferent, simply not a belligerent.'' Rusk explained that McClosky had meant the United States was a "non-belligerent'' but that neutrality did not mean "indifference.''[18]

The Soviet Union warned Israel that it would break relations unless Israel observed the U.N. cease-fire resolutions, and it further warned that "it goes without saying that the Soviet Government will consider and implement other necessary measures stemming from Israel's aggressive policy.'' While Israeli soldiers armed with machine guns and rocket launchers prayed at the Western Wall in Jerusalem, the Israeli government declared its willingness to accept a cease-fire if the enemy did the same. At the Western Wall, Moshe Dayan declared, "We have returned to the holiest of holy places, never to depart from it again.'' The Israelis held Sinai, with Sharm El-Sheik, and the West Bank, but the Arabs still refused to accept a cease-fire, and the major powers were saying the same things that they had been saying since before June 5. President Johnson declared that he was seeking peace in the Middle East, France proposed that an international declaration be issued making the Gulf of Eilat free to all ships, and the Soviet Union threatened Israel, and the British cautioned lest the Arabs be offended. Lots of talk. No action.

When the Soviets presented a cease-fire resolution, they called for the withdrawal of all forces to positions held prior to the war, but the Security Council did not agree. The resolution passed by the Security Council was general and unconditional. And as that resolution was passed on June 6, U.S. Ambassador Goldberg disclaimed any American complicity with Israeli military operations by inviting U.N. personnel on board U.S. aircraft carriers in the Mediterranean area.

On June 6, Israel responded to the Security Council's call for a

cease-fire by asking for direct negotiations with the Arabs.   The
victor called for peace.   Israel asked for man to man talks to clear up
mistrusts and misunderstandings.   But, as in the past, they said no.
Thanks to major power intervention and poor leadership among her
neighbors, Israel's differences with the Arabs were not eliminated.
On the contrary, they were deepened.   The Soviet Union reinvested
billions of dollars to rearm the Arabs, and the Arabs became more
recalcitrant.   The Soviets supported Arab terrorists and remained
silent when those terrorists ceaselessly committed acts of murder.

Israeli aircraft and torpedo boats attacked the U.S. radar-com-
munications ship *Liberty* that was apparently recording and reporting
the fighting in Sinai that June 8.   A number of American sailors were
killed and wounded, but Robert McNamara testified before the
Foreign Relations Committee that it had been an accident.   Israel was
to make reparations even though the American spy ship had refused
to identify itself, and had been reportedly interfering with Israeli
military activity in the Sinai.

In the afternoon of June 8, U Thant announced that the United
Arab Republic had accepted the cease-fire, but the Soviets confused
the situation still further by condemning the Israelis for "aggressive
activities" and insisting that Israel withdraw without any peaceful
settlement.   Throughout the U.N. debates, the Soviets attacked
Israel.   Federenko, who represented the Soviet Union, the very state
that had fostered aggression through its Hitler-Stalin pact of 1939,
charged Israel with Nazism.   Said Federenko on June 9: Israel fol-
lows "the bloody footsteps of Hitler's executioners...."   Israel must
be punished and she must "immediately, unconditionally withdraw
its troops...."

As Israeli soldiers cleared the Golan Heights, Johnson used every
diplomatic means to persuade Israel to conclude a cease-fire with
Syria because he feared possible Soviet intervention.   At 3 p.m. on
June 10, President Johnson received word that Israel would carry out
a cease-fire with Syria.

But the cease-fire did not come fast enough for the Soviets, and a
message came over the hot line from Kosygin: Israel must unconditionally stop its activities within the next hours or the Soviet Union
will take the "necessary actions, including military."   L.B.J. responded by sending the U.S. fleet to within 50 miles of the Syrian
coast.   Its distance was usually 100 miles, and Johnson told Kosygin

that a cease-fire would soon be concluded between Israel and Syria. The Soviets got the message.[19]

As the Soviets were unable to muster enough Security Council votes to declare Israel "the aggressor State" and order her immediate withdrawal to pre-June 5 lines, they called for a special General Assembly meeting to examine the Middle East situation. New York was hot and blistery that June 17, and the General Assembly debate was as unbearable as the weather. The Soviet-Arab coalition was ceaseless in its vicious attacks on Israel. But the Soviet-Arab alliance failed to obtain the resolution for which it hungered. They voted on the resolution paragraph-by-paragraph, and those sections that were anti-Israel were rejected. The paragraph which condemned Israel for "aggressive activities" and the occupation of parts of Egypt, Syria and Jordan was defeated by a vote of 36 in favor, 57 opposed and 23 abstentions. the paragraph demanding immediate ad unconditional withdrawal was defeated by a vote of 45 in favor, 48 opposed and 22 abstentions. And that which called on Israel to pay reparations was likewise defeated. The vote on that one was 34 in favor, 54 opposed and 28 abstentions.

Two days later, President Johnson presented a five-point program for peace in the Middle East:

> *First,* the recognized right of national life,
>
> *Second,* justice for the refugees,
>
> *Third,* innocent maritime passage,
>
> *Fourth,* limits on the wasteful and destructive arms race,
>
> *Fifth,* political independence and territorial integrity for all.

The President broadcasted the U.S. peace program while the U.N. fought over resolutions. The Soviets had been defeated in the General Assembly on one of their resolutions, but they did not give up. This time, they tried to get their way through a resolution submitted by Yugoslavia and 16 non-aligned states which called for the immediate and unconditional withdrawal of Israeli forces to pre-June 5 positions. But despite all the electioneering of the Soviet-Arab group, the Yugoslav resolution failed to muster the required two-thirds majority. There were 53 votes in favor, 46 opposed and 20 abstentions. A U.S.-backed Latin American resolution which called for the withdrawal of Israeli forces together with an end to Arab belligerency likewise failed to win the necessary two-thirds vote. The Middle East debate was shuffled back to the Security Council.

For a brief time, Israel was popular even within the closed circles of Washington's State and Defense departments. Israel had won the war against the Arabs and she had exposed and defeated the Soviets in the battlefield as well as in the U.N. Israel had captured billions of dollars worth of Soviet equipment and, while the Soviets supported the Arabs with equipment and words, they would not fight for them.

GLASBORO

The Soviet-Arab defeat was not permanent. The Soviet Union soon replaced the captured equipment and stationed its ships in Egyptian and Syrian ports. President Johnson, through his various communications, including the hot line messages and summit meetings at Glasboro State College in New Jersey, was unable to keep the Soviets from spreading their influence. The Israelis had won a war of survival and they had defeated Soviet might, but for the second time in ten years, the United States failed to take advantage of that fact.

At the conclusion of the first Johnson-Kosygin meeting on June 23, President Johnson announced that there would be another meeting in two days. After that second meeting, the two world leaders declared that their talks had been "very good and very useful." But what had they agreed to at Glasboro? According to Roger P. Davies, Deputy Assistant Secretary of State for Near Eastern and South Asian Affairs, "they agreed not intervene in the war."[20] From Johnson's memoirs, one learns that Kosygin had insisted Israel should go back to the original armistice lines and that the gulf of Eilat should be referred to the International Court of Justice. Kosygin maintained that unless the U.S. accepted his formula, there would be a war and a "very great war" at that. Arabs would fight with weapons if they had weapons, and if tney had none, they would fight with their bare hands. Johnson replied that if the Arabs would fight with weapons, "we would know where they got them." Then L.B.J. leaned forward and quietly told Kosygin: "Let us understand one another. I hope there will be no war. If there is a war, I hope it will not be a big war. If they fight, I hope they fight with fists and not with guns." The President concluded by saying that he hoped both the Soviet Union and the United States could keep out of any Middle East war because "if we do get into it, it will be a most serious matter."[21]

THE NOVEMBER 22, 1967 RESOLUTION

When the 22nd regular General Assembly session convened in September 1967, and Austria, Finland and Sweden submitted a proposal calling on the U.N. to again consider the Middle East situation, U Thant addressed the General Assembly with a pro-Arab and pro-Soviet statement. He admitted that Israel's request for direct peace talks was "most encouraging" but he did not believe such discussions were possible. He rejected Israel's assertion that the 1949 armistice agreements were no longer valid in view of the attacks by the Arab armies in June 1967, and he insisted that their validity and applicability had not been affected by the recent hostilities or by the 1956 war.

The Assembly debate raged on for weeks with no sign of progress. The issue was once again turned over to the Security Council, and there, India, Mali and Nigeria submitted a resolution which vaguely referred to the need to end the state of belligerency, respect for sovereignty, territorial integrity and political independence of all Middle Eastern states. Their main point was the withdrawal of Israel from all the lands "occupied as a result of the recent conflict." Their resolution was fully supported by the Arabs and the Soviets, but the United States rejected it. Ambassador Goldberg insisted that the 1949 armistice lines were provisional and based only on military considerations, and that they could be revised in the transition to peace. Neither the armistice lines nor the cease-fire lines of 1967 could be considered as permanent territorial boundaries. "Since such boundaries do not exist," said the U.S. representative, "they have to be established by the parties as part of the peace-making process." The Soviets, in turn, rejected the U.S. proposal for a return to mutually agreed "secure and recognized" boundaries. The British stepped in and brought together a resolution which was broad enough to allow each side to find it acceptable to its own views. The British resolution adopted the India-Mali-Nigeria provisions which referred to the "inadmissability of the acquisition of territory by war" and did not rule out the drawing up of newly agreed boundaries. Furthermore, the resolutions provided for: 1. "Withdrawal of Israeli armed forces from territories of recent conflict," but not from all such territories; 2. Termination of claims of states of belligerency and respect for and acknowledgement of the sovereignty, territorial integrity and political independence of every state in the area, and their right to live in peace within secure and recognized boundaries free from threats or acts of force; 3. Guaranteed freedom of navigation through international waterways in the area; 4. A just settlement of the refugee problem; 5. Guarantee of the territorial inviolability and political independence of every state in the area, through measures including the establishment of demilitarized zones. It concluded by requesting the Secretary General to designate a special representative to help "achieve a peaceful and accepted settlement in accordance with the provisions and principles in this resolution."

The United States explained its vote in favor of the resolution by asserting that "there had never been secure and recognized boundaries" in the Arab-Israeli conflict and that "secure boundaries could not be imposed from the outside." The Soviets interpreted the resolution to mean "withdrawal of Israeli forces from all conquered territories of the Arab States."

Israel believed that it could "live with" the resolution, but Syria rejected it altogether and other Arab states increased their support of the terrorists who sought the destruction of Israel.

In December 1967, U Thant appointed Dr. Gunnar Jarring, the Swedish Ambassador to the Soviet Union, as his special representative to establish peace in the Middle East. From his headquarters in Cyprus, he commuted to Cairo, Amman, Jerusalem, Beirut and New York. From December 1967 to December 1968, he visited Jerusalem twenty-two times. The Israelis felt that there had to be an agreement on all elements of the resolution and that representatives of the Arab governments concerned should meet with them. Jordan and Egypt rejected the Israeli position. They insisted on withdrawal first, and then they might talk with Israel.

Such was the Middle East discussions from 1967 to 1973. There would be Big-Two and later Big-Four talks, and various plans for peace, but peace was not to be had.

Israel retained its confidence in President Johnson even though he had not kept the Soviets out of the Mediterranean. Acting Premier Yigal Allon reflected that confidence when, on October 30, 1968, he said, "...the word of President Johnson in the six day war (had) played an historic role by warning the Soviet Union that her military intervention would cause a global confrontation." Allon believed that Johnson had taken "one of the boldest and most just decisions made by any President'' and that Johnson would help maintain the balance between Israel and the Arabs whenever it might be upset. The State Department soon threw cold water on Allon's optimism. While it concurred that the U.S. had a ''deep sense of obligation to see Israel survive as a nation'' the State Department contended that in the event of a joint Arab-Soviet attack against Israel, U.S. policy would be determined by the President in the light of events.

Yitzhak Rabin, Israel's Ambassador to the United States, did not share Allon's point of view. The former Israeli Chief of Staff felt that Israel could ''depend on nobody, nobody will solve our problems for us and nobody will raise a finger to aid us.''[22]

1 Abba Eban, *My Country* (New York, 1972), 197-98. Hereafter cited as Eban, *My Country*.

2 *Ibid.*; Ben Gurion, *Israel, A Personal History* (New York, 1970) 756-57. Hereafter cited as Ben Gurion, *Personal History;* Lyndon B. Johnson, *Vantage Point* (New York, 1971) 289-90. Hereafter cited as Johnson, *Vantage Point*.

3 Johnson, *Vantage Point*, 290; Eban, *My Country*, 200-01.

4 Ben Gurion, *Personal History*, 758.

5 Eban, *My Country*, 209-10.

6 Bar Zohar, *Embassies in Crisis*, (New Jersey, 1970) 124; Johnson, *Vantage Point*, 292-93.

7 Johnson, *Vantage Point*, 293-94; Eban, *My Country*, 210.

8 Bar Zohar, *Embassies In Crisis*, 125; Johnson, *Vantage Point*, 293-294.

9 Bar Zohar, *Embassies In Crisis*, 125.

10 *Ibid.*, 128.

11 *Ibid.*, 128-30.

12 Johnson, *Vantage Point*, 296,

13 For a fuller account of the fighting, consult such works as Yigal Allon, *The Making of Israel's Army* (New York, 1971) and Simon Peres, *David's Sling* (New York, 1970).

14 *The New York Times*, June 10, 1967.

15 Johnson, *Vantage Point*, 297-98.

16 Bar Zohar, *Embassies In Crisis*, 218-19.

17 Johnson, *Vantage Point*, 299.

Bar Zohar reports that McClosky had gotten the phrase from a briefing in which Eugene Rostow cautioned State Department officials against showing partiality to Israel. He told them to remember that America was ''neutral in word, thought and deed.'' See Bar Zohar, *Embassies In Crisis*, 220.

In an interview with Deputy Assistant Secretary for Near Eastern and South Asian Affairs, Roger P. Davies, I discovered that McClosky had come from a briefing session where the news of Israel's big victories over Egyptian skies had come in. "Everyone was over-joyed with the good news. We had been put out quite a bit by Egypt's actions in Yemen and we were happy that Egypt would not get a chance to do the same kind of thing across the Israeli border. Who knows what would have happened?" — Interview with Roger P. Davies, January 27, 1970, Washington, D.C.

18 Johnson, *Vantage Point*, 299.

19 Johnson, *Vantage Point*, 301-03.

According to a report of a former intelligence officer which appeared in the August 1972 edition of *Ramparts* magazine, the Soviets were preparing to make a troop drop over Israel, there was increased Soviet long-range bomber activity and their naval forces had been on the move.

20 Interview with Roger P. Davies, January 28, 1970.

21 Johnson, *Vantage Point*, 483-84.

22 *Jerusalem Post*, November 1, 1968.

Chapter VII

In Search of Peace

The United States' policy toward Israel has been based on sovereign self interest. U.S. Presidents supported Israel when they found it to be in the United States' best interest to do so. While Israel tried to pursue an independent policy based on its sovereign interest, it depended greatly upon U.S. support and it had to harken to American advice and pressures, even when that advice was not in Israel's best interest. Such is the History of U.S.-Israeli relations.

In 1972, Israel won a long-term commitment on arms from the U.S. This was an unprecedented event, even though the Soviet Union had been supplying Arab states such as Syria and Egypt on a long-term basis for some years. But before President Nixon and Israel reached that *detente*, a long and difficult road had to be traversed. This chapter deals with that long road from 1968 to 1972.

CONTINUED ARAB TERRORISM

In July, 1968, Arab terrorists hijacked an El Al passenger plane to Algiers. In December 1968, another El Al aircraft was attacked at the Athens airport by Arab terrorists. One passenger was killed and another wounded. On February 18, 1969, still another aircraft was attacked — this time in Zurich, Switzerland. Six persons were injured when four Arab terrorists raked the El Al plane with automatic fire and threw grenades and a bomb as it taxied for a take-off. An Israeli security guard on board the plane jumped out and killed one of the Arab terrorists. The other three were apprehended by airport personnel. Israel made no attempt to bring the Zurich atrocity before the Security Council because it realized that the Arab-Soviet dominated group would not rule legitimately.

Those attacks on Israeli aircraft in foreign airports were part of a general plan of terror which aimed to destroy Israel and tried to convince the world that there would be total destruction unless the Arabs had their way. Supplied and supported by Arab and Soviet governments, they claimed to be independent of established governments. Western news media glorified the assassins as heros. Egyptian President Nasser interpreted the Security Council resolution of November 22, 1967, as useful in forcing Israel to withdraw from occupied territories, but he added that the Council resolution was not enough to help eliminate Israel: "I must stress the glorious actions carried out by the Palestinian resistance forces...." He fully supported the terrorist goals of "sapping the enemy's strength and spilling its blood," and placed Egypt's resources "at the disposal of these organizations without condition or reservation."

Arab terrorism was not new to Israel. Before 1948, extremist elements of the Arab nationalist movement had used terrorism to impose their will on the moderates. In the 1920s and 1930s, Arab terrorism was preliminary to the invasion of the Arab armies in 1948, and it was an Arab policy of the 1950s as well as the 1960s. Terrorism was not new to the Jews. They had been pursued by murderers throughout history. Nor was the refusal of world organizations to express opposition to such terrorism new to the Jews either.

While the world seemed disturbed by the attacks on Israel, the U.N. was unwilling to condemn the terrorists. Israel was alone. For more than two decades, the U.N. proved unwilling or unable to ensure Israel's rights and to protect the lives of its citizens. As in the past, Israel discovered that it could depend only on itself.

On December 28, 1968, an Israeli task force landed at Beirut airport. Thirteen Arab civilian aircraft were destroyed causing some forty-four million dollars in damage, but no civilians were hurt. All Israelis returned safely to their base. After this retaliation against the Lebanese-based attacks on Israeli aircraft and passengers, Israel's so-called "friends" were the first to condemn her. The United States delegation led the Security Council condemnation of Israel, and as so often in the past, the only country that was for Israel, was Israel. It was as it had been on June 5, 1967, November 1956, May 1948, 1939, 1938, 1933.... Israel reminded the Security Council that unlike the Lebanese-based attacks, Israel had chosen not to take lives, but to strike against "inanimate objectives." In response to the charge that the Israeli action had been "disproportionate" to the Arab attacks, Israel's U.N. Ambassador Tekoah asked when Israel's action might be considered appropriate to the assault that preceded it. Would the Israeli action have been appropriate if the Arabs had succeeded in blowing up a plane with 50 passengers on board at Athens airport? When it was suggested that Israel pay reparations for the aircraft destroyed at Beirut, Tekoah asked who might pay for the loss of Israeli lives? Was the life of an Israeli engineer, on a U.N. mission, killed in Athens worth less than the metal, wire and upholstery destroyed in Beirut?

On December 31, 1968, the Security Council condemned Israel, but not the Arab terrorists and their supporters, and it warned Israel that if such acts were repeated, the Council "would have to consider further steps to give effect to its decisions." Tekoah advised the Council of its "moral, political and juridicial bankruptcy," but despite his eloquence, Israel was still very much alone.

During his 1968 Presidential campaign, Richard Nixon pronounced his support of Israel. He said that Israel was here to stay, that Israel could well take care of itself, but that the U.S. should provide her with the military edge, that the U.S. should establish its influence over the Arab world and that it should promote some sort of understanding with the Soviet Union concerning the Middle East. His words were many. He believed that the United States had supported Israel in the past and would do so in the future because the Israelis had shown those qualities which Americans admire most: "guts, patriotism, idealism, a passion for freedom." And while he did not believe Israel should take formal possession of the administered territories, he would not ask Israel "to surrender vital bargaining counters in the absence of a genuine peace and effective guarantees."

Once Nixon defeated Democrat Hubert H. Humphrey, in the national elections, he sent William Scranton on a fact-finding mission to the Middle East. This was to be Nixon's first turnabout on his foreign policy campaign promises. It would start with a call for an "even-handed policy in the Middle East" and it would end with a betrayal of Israel. Throughout his travels in the Arab world and Israel, Scranton would claim that the "impression in the Middle East is widespread that the U.S. is only interested in Israel." He insisted that the U.S. should take into consideration the feelings of all persons and all countries in the Middle East and not necessarily espouse one nation over the other. Perhaps this was Nixon's way of showing that there was nothing sacred about past American policies and that he would not submit to public pressures on foreign policy matters.[1] Whatever his motivations may have been, the Scranton statements were not well received at home, and on December 11, his aides sought to disassociate Nixon from Scranton's remarks. Said Press Secretary Ronald Ziegler: "His remarks are Scranton remarks, not Nixon remarks."

To those with a knowledge of recent history, the scenario was familiar. Recall that when Eisenhower became President in 1953, there had been much talk about Truman having shown favoritism toward Israel, and that a more "impartial policy" was needed. Scranton talked about a "more even-handed policy." Dulles, in 1953, declared that the U.S. had to assuage Arab resentment caused by Israel's establishment.

But Israel publicly welcomed Nixon's desire to improve U.S. relations with the Arabs. Perhaps the Israelis thought the United States might persuade the Arabs to talk peace. General Moshe Dayan said that he saw nothing wrong in Nixon's policies. He said that Israel wanted to purchase arms from the U.S., and he hoped America would maintain a strong position so as to deter the Soviet Union from bringing war to the Middle East. But Nixon would not be forthcoming with those arms. He would pursue a policy that would seek to immobilize Israel while the Arabs prepared to destroy the Jewish State. The same Nixon posture would prevent Israel from forcing the Arabs to surrender during the October 1973 war, and would ultimately lead to a nuclear confrontation between the U.S. and the Soviet Union.

The New York Times observed that Scranton had unnecessarily complicated Nixon's approach to "an issue of enormous sensitivity." It referred to the dangers of "sending amateur envoys to explosive areas." Nixon would deny that he wanted to dictate to Israel, but his actions contradicted his denials. On January 27, 1969, he spoke of the need for new initiatives and new leadership on the part of the U.S. in order to cool down Middle East tensions. He called the Middle East "a powder keg." Therefore, it was "time to turn to the left now."

BIG POWER TALKS

During the last months of his Administration, Johnson had moved toward joint intervention with the Soviet Union in bringing about a settlement in the Middle East. Nixon continued Johnson's interventionist policy. Among the ideas considered by Nixon was a plan for Israeli withdrawal from the Golan Heights and Sinai and for some "minor adjustments" on the Jordanian frontier. The plan envisaged demilitarization of the Sinai and a ten mile strip within Israeli territory running south from the Gaza Strip but stopping north of the port of Eilat.[2]

On January 16, 1969, France proposed Big Four talks to bring a settlement. The U.S. responded by calling for preliminary bilateral talks among the Big Four. Ostensibly, such talks were to assist Gunnar Jarring's mission, but as it happened, they eased Jarring's mission out of existence. Israel was wary. From Israel's viewpont, there could be no "peace by proxy."[3]

Foreign Minister Eban said that such intervention diverted attention from the need "to base peace on the initiative and the agreement of the parties, of the governments of the Middle East, who alone will fashion the Middle Eastern future." The Soviet Union and France favored the Arabs and did not have a balanced, even-handed attitude. Big Four intervention would make peace unattainable.[4]

Israel likewise rejected the notion of an international U.N. peace force on Israeli soil. In 1967, there had been a "situation in which peace was alleged to depend upon a U.N. Force, and it disappeared overnight like a fire brigade broke away when the fire broke out." Eban rejected the notion of trying to get justice from the U.N. because no resolution which was not congenial to the Arabs would ever be adopted by that body. This was because the Arabs always had their brothers and cousins in the Security Council and even if the majority of the Security Council agreed, the Soviets would use their veto to see to it that "we don't get justice."

In the middle of March, Eban went to see Secretary of State Rogers and tried to persuade the U.S. to abandon its big power initiatives for a Middle East settlement. He asked that the negotiations be left up to Israel and the Arab states, but the Nixon plan called for a Big Four effort. The major powers were to develop an outline of a settlement package for Israel and the Arab states which Gunnar

Jarring would present to them.[5]

Big Four talks were a waste of time. Nasser called for another holy war: "We have declared our principles — no negotiations, no peace, no relinquishing one inch of Arab land and no bargaining over Palestinian rights."

While Egypt called for war, Israel rejected an imposed peace: "Israel entirely opposes the plan to convene the representatives of states that lie outside the Middle East in order to prepare recommendations concerning the region." The way to peace was through direct negotiations. By such diplomacy, maintained the Israelis, "agreed, secure and recognized boundaries will be laid down in the peace treaties." Israel was prepared to negotiate "without prior conditions from any side." But in the absence of peace treaties, Israel would maintain its position "as determined by the cease-fire and will consolidate her position in accordance with the vital needs of her security and development."[6]

Nixon continued his pressure. His Secretary of State insisted that if the Big Four agreed on a formula for a Middle East settlement, the governments in the area would have to "think long and hard before they turned it down." Almost in the same breath, Secretary Rogers insisted that no settlement would be imposed.

The Jarring mission was hampered by the major powers, and the Arabs stiffened their position on the boundaries question. Some Arab representatives went so far as to call for the restoration of the 1947 Partition Plan. Israeli Ambassador Tekoah called attention to the growing tension along the cease-fire lines. He attributed the difficulties to the Arab belief that if they made enough trouble, the Big Four would act to force a settlement on Israel.[7] Once again, Israel issued a statement opposing the Big Four interventions: "If the Jarring mission has not, to date, met with success, it is because Arab Governments have found avenues of escape away from a direct peace commitment with Israel." The Jarring mission lost its purpose as defined by the Security Council resolution because it was obscured again and again by pluralism of initiatives from outside the region.

In September 1969, Prime Minister Meir met with Nixon hoping to obtain long-range military and economic commitments.[8] She did not succeed. Nixon urged a continuation of Big Power talks so as to avoid the mistakes that might involve the great powers in a war started by smaller states.[9] Rogers presented a set of proposals for the Middle East which conceded that a Middle East peace should be negotiated by the parties themselves, and he called for a return to the 1967 frontiers with changes limited to insubstantial alterations required for mutual security; settlement of the refugee problem, freedom of navigation in the Suez Canal and the Straits of Tiran; and the settlement of Jerusalem's status.

The Rogers formulas failed to bring peace, and they were rejected by both Israel and the Arabs. Israel rejected his plans because he disregarded the need for secure and recognized boundaries, prejudiced Israel's security on the question of refugees and Jerusalem, and because it failed to provide for any obligation on the Arab states to discontinue their state of war and their support of terrorist activities. Golda Meir found the Big Four talks one-sided. The United States had submitted ten to fifteen plans of peace since 1967, but the Soviets had just one. If she were a Soviet leader, Meir said, she would do "exactly the same." The Soviets "sit there and say... 'This is too pro-Israel. This we can't accept,' and in another month or even two weeks there's another paper and the Russians say, 'This?' and turn it back." Each "new proposal encouraged the Arabs to increase their military activity across the borders." How could this possibly lead to peace? Meir found nothing in Rogers' proposals which called upon the Arabs to extend formal recognition to Israel. There was no reference as to how many refugees Israel had to take back. Rogers seemed to propose that all the refugees should be taken back by Israel, even those who had "never stepped into a refugee camp," and had established themselves in Cairo, Damascus and Beirut. Mrs. Meir found that instead of encouraging Israel and Jordan to negotiate a refugee settlement, the Rogers plan encouraged the Arabs to refuse a reasonable settlement. Israel likewise rejected the notion of the internationalization of Jerusalem. As Meir put it:

"Israel won't accept this. We're not going to commit suicide.
"That isn't what we're living here for and what thousands have died for. Nobody in the world can make us accept it."[10]

Rogers rejected Meir's charge that his proposals amounted to an appeasement of the Arabs. He admitted that Israel might have some reason to be "concerned" and to "disagree" with U.S. policy, but the U.S. had to conduct its "policy in a way that we think is best for our national interest."

Major power interventionist diplomacy failed, and by early 1970 Nixon went public with reassurances that he would not abandon Israel. He insisted that his Administration had no intention of imposing a peace on the parties and he declared his intention of helping Israel with its weapons requests.

Nixon's message, while vague, reassured Israel's supporters that Nixon was concerned with Israel's needs for peace and security. Meir now recalled that when she had seen Nixon, he revealed a sympathetic understanding of Israel's desire that peace be achieved "through a freely negotiated agreement between the parties of the conflict...." Meir supported the President's remarks, but the Arabs did not, and in order to quiet Arab apprehensions, U.S. officials reassured them on January 27, that Nixon's message to American Jewish leaders did not in any way invalidate the American Middle East proposals as enunciated by Rogers on December 9. Furthermore, the Arabs were advised that no decision had been made on a four month old Israeli request for additional military and economic aid. To some, it sounded like the F.D.R. days. They recalled how Roosevelt would tell the Jews that he would help them re-establish their homeland in Palestine, and then he would inform the Arabs that nothing would be done without their consent. It seemed as if things had not changed much in forty years.

In response to those who claimed his diplomacy was two-faced, Nixon said on January 30 that "we are neither pro-Arab nor pro-Israel. We are pro-peace." He promised to make a decision "within the next thirty" on Israel's request for additional Phantom and Skyhawk jets. But it would take Nixon longer than thirty days. Fifty-two days later, his Secretary of State announced that the President had decided not to make a binding decision. That meant that Israel would not get the jets; but a promise was made that the jets would be delivered when in the President's judgement there was a need for them. That was Nixon's unilateral first step in his plan to limit the arms race in the Middle East. But other states like the Soviet Union and France continued supplying the Arabs with all manner of weapons.

During his news conference of March 21, Nixon announced that Rogers would present the U.S. decision on the sale of arms to Israel in two days, and he again talked at length about his goals for peace. That Monday, Rogers declared that the U.S. would not sell Israel the planes, and then he promised another peace plan for the Middle East. Nixon viewed the SAM-3 missiles and Soviet military units stationed in Egypt as "defensive" rather than an "offensive" improvement of Egypt's military posture. Even after Israel revealed conclusive evidence that "Soviet pilots were flying operational missions from military installations under their control in Egypt, and that the Russians were manning SAM-3 missiles"[11] Nixon still failed to provide Israel with the necessary weapons. On June 25, Rogers recognized that the Soviets had jeopardized the balance of power, but still refused to publicly indicate whether, or how, the U.S. would support its pledge to maintain the balance of power.

From the spring of 1969 to the summer of 1970, there had been a war of attrition on the Gulf of Suez between Egypt and Israel. On August 4, Israel accepted the U.S. peace initiative which included a three month cease-fire along the Suez Canal. But as soon as the cease-fire went into effect, the Egyptians reinforced their positions in violation of that cease-fire. When Israel provided the U.S. with reconnaissance photos showing the Egyptian violations, State and Defense department officials claimed that those pictures were inconclusive.[12]

And there was trouble with Syria again. Jordan tried to eliminate the *fedayeen* menace from within its border and Syria reacted with an invasion of Jordan. War was expected in the Middle East.[13]

Rogers saw Soviet Ambassador Dobrynin and the State Department announced that the Soviets had been asked to remove the Syrians from Jordan. Nixon considered sending U.S. Air Force and Marines into Jordan, but he preferred to let the Israelis contain the Syrians with U.S. air power protecting the Israeli rear from Egyptian and Soviet intervention. Close contact was maintained between American and Israel intelligence. When the Soviets and Syrians realized that the U.S. and Israel meant business, they backed down. The U.S. and Israel saved Jordan in 1970.[14]

Later in September, Nixon visited American forces in the Mediterranean and noted that he had come to see "the mightiest military force which exists in the world on any ocean." Addressing American sailors on the aircraft carrier *U.S.S. Saratoga*, the President said that "never has American power...been used with more effectiveness" than it had been in recent weeks in the Middle East.[15] Since Israel was unable to obtain a rollback of Egypt's expanded missile positions along Suez, it tried again to obtain necessary arms, and the U.S. guarantee of help in case Soviet pilots in Arab states became more directly involved in the fighting.

The Soviet entrenchments of missiles along Suez and Soviet in-spired Syrian attacks against Jordan convinced Nixon that it was not possible to achieve a comprehensive agreement with the Soviets regarding the Middle East. It was to the Unites States' advantage to support Israel. The President pledged his support for Israel's security needs, but it still seemed that he had made no specific pledges of new arms deals or of a security guarantee. On December 11, Moshe Dayan, the Israeli Defense Minister, went to Washington and asked for long-term arms supplies. Dayan met with the President, Secretary of State Rogers and Secretary of Defense Melvin Laird. He talked with them about Israel's peace terms, the means of dealing with increased Soviet involvement in Egypt's defense, and future arms sales to Israel.[16] When Dayan spoke before a gathering of the United Jewish Appeal, he praised the President for having "kept every word he told us since he came to power...."

Reassuring Israel that the U.S. would not permit Israel to become diplomatically isolated, Nixon persuaded Israel to return to the negotiations, which had been broken off soon after they had begun on August 25. But Meir, in an interview with James Reston, was "decidedly pessimistic" about the chances for peace. She felt that even if there was some hope for a settlement, it all would take a very long time and she blamed the Soviets. She compared the Soviet attitude toward Israel with Germany's moves against Czechoslovakia in 1938; but she pointed to one major difference, Israel would actively defend itself.

> You know the Russians....They don't stop at anything. I think they are very careful - it isn't true that they just rush into something. First, they put in one foot - how's the water? The next one goes in. That is their mentality, that's how they work, and I am horrified to see how the free world sits back.

Meir reiterated the need for ongoing agreements with the U.S. regarding arms sales and diplomatic support:

> The other side has constant flow of arms. It is not interrupted for a day, and it isn't just more of the same - they did not have missiles a year and a half ago, and now we know...

there are surface-to-surface missiles of the Frog - 7 type.
They...have...one hundred percent backing for anything in
territorial problems, political problems that the Egyptians
will put on the table.
...is it too much for us to ask from the U.S., that the supply
of arms needed for our defense be based on an ongoing
relationship, without the necessity for us to negotiate each
time for additional shipments?[17]

The talks continued. The Arabs and their supporters insisted that
Israel withdraw first, but Israel maintained that there must be a
contractual peace before any withdrawal.

On February 6, 1972, the U.S. announced its decision to sell Israel
some 42 F-4 Phantom jets, and 90 A-4 Skyhawks. The peace talks
continued, but so did the arms race, Arab terrorism, oil blackmail
and the fears of another war.

Israel's position was perhaps better in the early part of 1973 than it
had been in May 1967. The Soviets had apparently withdrawn from
Egypt, but they had not abandoned their goal of eventual world
conquest, and the Middle East was still part of the world. Israel
continued to face great political, economic and military pressures
from friend and foe alike. Four wars with the Arabs and their
supporters, and the experiences of the Jews during World War II,
taught Israel that unless it provided for its own security no one
would.

Israel had insisted that before there would be any withdrawal from
any of the administered territories there had to be a contractual peace
with the Arab states. How long Israel could maintain that stance was
anybody's guess. It depended not only on Israel's determination and
ability to defend itself, but also upon the complexity of international
relations.

Israel could expect to have U.S. support for as long as the U.S.
considered it to be in its sovereign interests to aid Israel. Every
President since Roosevelt pursued relations with the Zionists and
Israel on those terms. While some American Presidents like Truman
may have been more inclined to assist Israel than some officials in
the State Department, the primary concern of the Presidents was the
sovereignty and self-interests of the U.S.A. Israel continued her
search for self-reliance as well as her search for friendship among all
the nations of the world. The events of October 1973 revealed how
poorly she fared in both efforts.

1 Henry Brandon, *The Retreat of American Power*, (New York, 1973), 106-107, Hereafter cited as Brandon, *Retreat of American Power*.

2 *The New York Times*, January 31, 1969.

3 *Ibid.*, February 6, 1969.

4 NBC's "Meet the Press," March 16, 1969.

5 *The New York Times*, March 21, 1969.

6 *Ibid.*, March 31, 1969.

8 *Ibid.*, September 26, 1969.

9 *Ibid.*

10 *Ibid.*, October 25, 1970.

11 *Ibid.*, December 23, 1969.

12 *Ibid.*, April 30, 1970.
After President Nixon's description of the Middle East as another Balkans before the outbreak of World War I, stories were published that Israel had built its own nuclear weapons. On July 4, 1970, Jerry Greene reported in the *Daily News* that the White House knew Israel had at least 10 well developed and tested guided missiles with a range of 280 miles. These, he reported, were constructed for the delivery of atomic weapons. If Israel had not already put together the nuclear explosives for the missiles, technical experts felt Israel was capable of doing so speedily. Those same experts estimated that Israel would not use the atomic weapons unless she were in a real crunch. Israel might either announce possession of the atomic weapons and the intent to use them, or she might begin a series of tests.
The missiles were developed by AVIONS MARCEL, a French company with the help of Israeli scientists at a cost of $25 million. See *Daily News*, July 4, 1970.

13 *New York Times*, August 19, 1970.

14 Brandon, *Retreat of American Power*, 128-139.

15 *Ibid.*

16 *The New York Times*, December 12, 1970.

17 *Ibid.*, December 27, 1970.

Chapter VIII

October Days 1973

It was October 6, 1973, and it was Yom Kippur in the Jewish calendar. While Israel was at prayer, the Arabs attacked. How did it happen that Israel chose to wait for Egypt and Syria to attack when it had information regarding Egyptian and Syrian war plans? Why did Israel disregard its essential need for a pre-emptive strike when its neighbors amassed thousands of tanks, artillery, missiles and hundreds of thousands of men along the borders? Was it because Israel thought the Arab mobilization was just another false alarm, two of which had only recently cost Israel millions of dollars? Was it as one Israeli official claimed that "if we had responded to every Arab mobilization it could have driven us crazy?"[1]

Was Israel misinformed by her intelligence services, and by her friends and allies? Or was Israel forced to wait it out by the Big Powers? Had the U.S. warned Israel that if it struck first it would get no political, military or economic assistance? Is it possible that Israeli leaders agreed to be a "little" defeated so that Egypt and Syria might recover "Face," the Sinai east bank, and parts of the Golan Heights? Was this part of the Soviet-American 1973 detente?

Yigal Allon, the Deputy Prime Minister by the time of the Yom Kippur War, had described the need for a pre-emptive strike in his book, *The Making of the Israeli Army*. As he put it, Israel could not afford to stand by while the Arabs built up their offensive striking position. Israel could not afford to behave towards the Arabs as if they were at peace. The anticipatory counter-attack could be launched months, weeks, days and even hours before the Arab attack. But Israel had to "forestall" a future Arab attack.[2]

Since conditions in early October 1973 were so volatile, why did Israel fail to respond? There have been many explanations offered, but no satisfactory answers. During and after the war, Israeli spokesmen said they sat back because they wanted the world to see that the Arabs were responsible for the war. "We could have destroyed them," said Simcha Dinitz, Israel's Ambassador to the U.S., "when the Egyptians and Syrians were sitting like ducks, but we wanted everyone to be sure this time that Israel had done everything to prevent war."[3] Or as Prime Minister Meir said during an interview on October 28, 1973, "we could have talked till our faces turned blue and no one would have believed" that Israel had acted in self-defense.

State Department spokesman Robert McClosky said that the U.S. had received various reports from a variety of sources over several weeks that Egypt and Syria were building up their military forces. But he claimed that the reports had not been definitive and that investigations by U.S. intelligence indicated the Arab build-up had been "defensive in nature and not such that would presage imminent military action."

A report had reached the State Department on Friday night, October 5, that indicated the buildup was "more than defensive" and by 6 a.m., New York time, October 6, the U.S. had learned that military action was "imminent.

OCTOBER 3

Prime Minister Meir was back in Israel. She had met with Austrian Prime Minister Kreisky in Strasbourg, France, in order to persuade him to reopen Austrian facilities for Soviet Jewish refugees. Days before, when the Israeli Ambassador to France had urged her to return to Israel because of the Arab military[4] buildup, she insisted that she had to stay so as to persuade Kreisky. The "Russian immigrants are so important to Israel," said Meir, "that if there is one percent, or even half a percent, chance of changing Kreisky's mind, I must try."[5] Why did Meir choose to remain away from Israel at this crucial time? Was it only because of the Russian Jews? This remains one of the many unanswered questions of the Yom Kippur War.

In recent autobiographies published by Mr. Dayan and Mrs. Meir, we learn very little about all this. Perhaps the most important thing about both books is that they omit almost all reference to the pressures imposed by the U.S. on Israel not to pre-empt. They expressed their gratefulness for the supplies that came, but hardly a word about the role played by the U.S. in early October 1973.[6]

Meir consulted with some of her Cabinet and advisors on the military and political situation. Among those present were Israel Galili, Minister without portfolio; David Elazar, Chief of Staff, Moshe Dayan, Minister of Defense; Yigal Allon, Deputy Prime Minister and General Arye Shalev, Research Assistant to the Director of Military Intelligence. The Syrian and Egyptian military build-ups were discussed, but they were apparently viewed as similar to those of January, May and September 1973. Shalev's intelligence report concluded that the possibility of an Egyptian-Syrian war "did not seem likely."[7] Israeli intelligence had a full picture of Egypt's attack strategy, but the Israeli officials seemed to believe Egypt would strike only after it acquired aircraft capable of striking deep into Israel. Meir said she would place the situation on the agenda of the regular Cabinet meeting scheduled for October 7.[8]

OCTOBER 4

Two days before the Arab attack, every effort was made by Meir to play down the Arab threat to Israel's survival. When she reported to the Defense and Foreign Affairs committees of Parliament on her European trip, she made no reference to the Arab troop concentrations. Later that same day, she publicly attacked the opposition party for its persistent forecasts of Arab attacks. "Not one bit of the black prophesies of Gahal have come true. Why," Meir taunted, "don't the Gahal people have the courage to admit their error?" While she thus castigated Israeli members of Parliament for being concerned for Israel's future, Israeli military intelligence reports indicated that Soviet families were leaving Egypt and Syria. "Red Alert!" At a special Zahal (Israeli Defense Forces) military staff meeting late in the night, it was decided to issue an alert the next morning for the regular army. But there was no mobilization of the reserves.[9]

OCTOBER 5

An Israeli Army spokesman issued a statement that Israeli forces were "following with attention events on the Egyptian side of the Suez Canal and all steps have been taken to prevent the possibility of a surprise on the part of the Egyptians."

Reportedly, when General Ariel Sharon was summoned to the Southern Command headquarters at 11:30 a.m., he examined the air reconnaissance photos and told his division officers that there would be "war in one or two days." The pictures revealed a large-scale build-up of water-crossing equipment on the western side of the Canal.[10]

While Generals Dayan, Elazar and Zeira met, reports came in of large-scale Soviet transports arriving in Cairo and Damascus with heavy weapons. Syrian guns were redeployed from a defensive to an offensive position pointing south into Israeli settlements. Israeli Air Force reconnaissance flights over Egypt revealed that the Egyptians were moving up troops, and water-crossing equipment to the Canal area. Holiday leaves were canceled for the regular Israeli forces and the reserve mobilization machinery was likewise alerted. On its own initiative, the Israeli Air Force called up its reserves. Despite all this, official Israeli intelligence still maintained that there was "little likelihood" of war. Dayan believed there would be an attack, but he seemed unsure as to what kind it would be. Defense officials met with Meir and other Cabinet people.[11]

Cabinet ministers reviewed both fronts while Generals Elazar and Zeira repeated their doubts that war would break out. General Elazar stressed the experience of previous build-ups, and that American intelligence also considered war unlikely. The Premier was encouraged by the reports that indicated war was unlikely after all. She planned to present the matter at the October 7 Cabinet meeting.[12]

Israeli leadership seemed indecisive, and American intelligence reports played down the danger of the situation, but the Soviets fanned the flames of war just as they had done in 1956 and in 1967. On October 3, 1973, *Izvestia* claimed that Israel was "deliberately demonstrating its military power and reliance on American support" with the aim of destroying Arab unity and to force them to capitulate singly.[13] Two days later, Soviet radio announced that Israeli troops were concentrating "in the area of the Lebanese frontier and the cease-fire line with Syria" and that Israel was stepping up its "war preparations."[14] The Soviet campaign warning of an imminent attack by Israel was not only similar to that of 1967, but indicated that the Soviet Union had advance knowledge of Arab plans to make war. The Soviet Union was preparing the background for future claims that would place responsibility for the war on Israel.

OCTOBER 6

In the early morning hours, the phones of Israel's chief military and political leaders were busy, Around 4 a.m., Elazar received a call from Zeira. Israeli agents had obtained copies of Arab war plans which called for an attack by 6 p.m., Israeli time. Elazar called Dayan and demanded full mobilization and a pre-emptive air attack at least in the Golan area. Dayan was opposed and insisted that only the Prime Minister could approve such action. He agreed to suggest it to Meir. The Prime Minister likewise opposed mobilization and pre-emption. At 6 a.m., Dayan met with Elazar at Tel Aviv headquarters. There was additional information regarding the Arab war plans. Intelligence had picked up radio traffic patterns of Syrian units preparing for war. Syrian soldiers were calling relatives in Lebanon advising them not to visit Syria for the weekend. Elazar called for full mobilization. In view of the late hour, Elazar felt, Israel would have to give ground and then counterattack. Dayan disagreed. Israeli forces could repel the attack and no counterattack would be necessary. Dayan believed that only a minimum of reserves would have to be called.

At 8 a.m., the generals were at Meir's home. Elazar again called for full mobilization and a pre-emptive air strike. Meir and Dayan rejected Elazar's recommendations. Dayan argued that an air strike would only disrupt Arab preparations for a few hours and the pilots would have to fly against a lethal missile screen. Meir seemed plagued by the fear that Israel would be left without friends if it struck first, but she gave Elazar permission to initiate partial mobilization. U.S. Secretary of State Kissinger seemed more concerned with a possible Israeli pre-emptive strike than an Egyptian-Syrian onslaught. He had intelligence information detailing how Arab "defensive formations" had been transformed into offensive dispositions, but he sent Israel a presidential entreaty not to start the war.

In the afternoon, the Israeli Cabinet met. Allon and Sapir were still not there. It seemed that when Allon was contacted by Cabinet Secretary Arnon, he asked if the situation was urgent, in which case he would take a helicopter back. But Arnon told him that it was not urgent, and so Allon drove from his kibbutz to Tel Aviv. Sapir learned how serious the situation was during Yom Kippur services as he saw his cantor and other members of the congregation leave for reserve duty. Sapir then called the Cabinet Secretary and discovered that the Cabinet was in session discussing imminent war.

Why had Arnon taken it so easy? Was it part of a Meir and Dayan plan to make the Arabs think that Israel was unaware of their war plans?

At the Cabinet meeting, Meir advised those present that there was need for mobilization, but she still rejected Elazar's recommendation for a pre-emptive strike. She recalled the political difficulties Israel had faced during the Six Day War. "This time it has to be crystal clear who began, so we won't have to go around the world convincing people our cause is just," said Meir. She would later explain that "...had the situation not been clear beyond the shadow of a doubt regarding who began hostilities I doubt whether the vital equipment received...would have flowed in as it did...."[15]

By 10 a.m., the decision was made to declare full mobilization of the reserves. This was six hours after there was clear evidence that war was imminent, and only four hours before Egypt and Syria would attack. United States Ambassador Kenneth Keating was called in by Mrs. Meir, and when he was told that Israel had "proof" that Egypt and Syria were planning to attack at 6 p.m., Keating expressed concern as to whether Israel would "strike first?"

"Emphatically not," was Meir's reply. Keating warned the Prime Minister that if Israel struck first, the U.S. would feel unable to resupply her. Meir asked Keating to inform President Nixon, the Soviet Union and the Arabs that Israel did not plan to strike first. Is it possible that the Arabs were informed that Israel knew of their plans to attack at 6 p.m.? Or was it, as some have explained, that the Arabs wanted to have the advantage of the sun? Why did they change to 2 p.m.? Matti Golan, author of *The Secret Conversations of Henry Kissinger* claimed that "no one knows where the assumption of a 6 p.m. attack came from."[16]

News accounts of the day tell us that at on October 6 at 6 a.m., New York time, Kissinger was awakened with the news of a possible war. He would later claim that the U.S. made "no demarche to either side before October," because all the intelligence at his disposal indicated there was not going to be a war. He claimed that there had been "no reason to give any advice to any of the participants because we did not believe - nor...did the Israeli Government - that an attack was imminent."[17] But by May 1973, Kissinger had detailed State Department reports based on the Egyptian battle plans secretly gathered by U.S. intelligence "predicting an offensive in the early autumn."[18] And in September, he had the Syrian war plans; but, according to Tad Szulc of *The New York Times*, Washington had "no thought of launching aerial reconnaissance over Egypt and Syria to determine their military deployment."[19] That was most peculiar behavior. According to Kissinger's public recollections, the U.S. made major efforts from 6 a.m. to 9 a.m. to prevent the outbreak of hostilities. Why hadn't Kissinger acted before that time, before the fighting had broken out? According to *London Sunday Times* correspondents, he had CIA   information at least 24 hours before the outbreak of war that Egypt and Syria would attack Israel. If Kissinger had been so interested in averting war, why did he wait so long? Could it be that he wanted to set up the Israelis for a defeat? Could it be that some Israeli leaders were ready to accept defeat, at least a temporary setback, so as to bolster Arab morale and bring the Arabs to the peace talks?

What of President Nixon's position? So far, we have only the word of Kissinger, and various secondary accounts. In his television interviews with David Frost, and in his memoirs, the ex-President did not reveal anything concerning those early days in October. According to Kissinger, the President "was convinced that we had ...first to end hostilities in a manner that would enable us to make a major contribution to removing the conditions that have produced four wars between Arabs and Israelis in the last 25 years." Those wars between Arabs and Israelis were to be ended. But what did he mean by "to end hostilities in a *manner* that would enable us to make a major contribution?" Did that word "manner" imply to enable Egypt and Syria to win at least a little?

It is unlikely that the war could have turned out better for the Egyptians and Syrians if the U.S. and U.S.S.R. or some other international force had written and directed the scenario of the Yom Kippur 1973 War.

Israel was alone. The U.S., Israel's main source of military equipment, had refused to sell her weapons to counter the ultra-modern, Soviet-built missile system which was furnished Egypt and Syria. Israel had no equipment with which to combat Soviet missiles. It did not have anything with which to combat the anti-tank missiles which were carried into battle by Arab infantrymen. As

Defense Minister Dayan put it on October 20, 1973: "What was lacking at the front was, first of all, certain types of equipment, and here perhaps someone should do some soul searching - maybe the Americans - for refusing to sell us certain types of armament. I am referring mainly to personal anti-tank weapons and other types of arms....we lack certain equipment, and the people who are providing it in the U.S. are bargaining whatever it is that we are lacking - so and so much a quarter of a plane more or less, delivery a day or so later. Now we are receiving equipment from the U.S. but they are sending from their heads not from their hearts."[21] S.L.A. Marshall and Winston Churchill, Jr., in their reports, supported Dayan's assertion that Israel had asked for certain sophisticated weapons, but that the U.S. had refused to sell that equipment.[22]

Egypt held the initiative. The Syrians broke through some Israeli defenses, but Meir reported that "Israel's position was about par for the course so far." What was that supposed to mean? Kissinger preferred to "let the boys play awhile."[23] That play would cost Israel a generation of young men. While American diplomats were so generous with Israeli and Arab lives, they advised the British to discontinue their efforts to bring about a cease-fire. At the same time, he held on to a policy of not providing Israel with needed supplies. It seemed to be part of a plan to have Israel defeated, at least a little bit. Israeli Minister Mordechai Shalev approached Joseph Sisco, Assistant Secretary for Near Eastern Affairs, while military attache Major General Mordechai Gur contacted Pentagon sources for additional supplies. The Americans said no.

OCTOBER 8

While reports indicated that the Soviets informed Nixon of their desire to limit the conflict, the U.S.S.R. representative at the U.N. refused to go along with a U.S. sponsored Security Council resolution for cease-fire. This was to be the Soviet, and the U.N. position, for as long as Egypt and Syria were having military successes.

Zahal struck back at Egyptian and Syrian forces. Chief of Staff General David Elazar announced: 'We have begun the destruction of the Egyptian Army," and "We are attacking the enemy wherever necessary."

Again, Israel requested supplies. Ambassador Dinitz made the request to Kissinger. The Secretary of State gave Dinitz some evasive answers.[24] Nixon and Kissinger preferred not to provide Israel with assistance. They preferred enhanced relations with the Soviets and the Arabs, and believed that arms shipments to Israel would damage relations with them. Kissinger supplied Dinitz with words of reassurance, and advised the Soviets of U.S. unwillingness to resupply Israel.[25] Next day, Dinitz went to see Kissinger again. This time he refused to accept Kissingerian equivocations on Israel's request for tanks, artillery and electronic equipment to counteract the Soviet missiles. Kissinger told Dinitz that Nixon agreed to resupply Israel. Dinitz believed that the necessary instructions had been transmitted to the Pentagon, and he sent Gur to the Pentagon with a shopping list. When Gur arrived at the Pentagon, he was informed that export licenses were needed. These, he was told, would have to be arranged by Kissinger. So the Pentagon sent the Israelis back to Kissinger. Catch-22.

At this point, Meir advised Dinitz that she wanted to travel to the U.S. incognito and talk with Nixon. When Dinitz transmitted this to Kissinger, he appeared totally out of control. Kissinger insisted that since such a visit could not be kept secret, it might encourage Soviet intervention. He tried to reassure Dinitz that the supplies question would soon be settled, perhaps within a few hours.[26] But it took more than a few days.

OCTOBER 9

Israeli units opened major counterattacks on two broad fronts. The Syrian and Egyptian armies were thrown back. There were heavy Israeli air attacks against enemy military airfields, missile sites and other military targets deep inside Egypt and Syria. Enemy resistance was heavier than expected. As Major General Aharon Yariv, special advisor to the Chief of Staff put it: "...we have been able to redress the situation, but there is still a way ahead of us which will not be easy."[27]

OCTOBER 10

Israel abandoned the Bar Lev Line, a series of fortifications facing the west bank of the Suez Canal, and it formed a new line three to five kilometers back, facing the Egyptian forces. Most of the Golan Heights were cleared of Syrians. While Syrian "strategic targets" in Damascus, and the oil refineries of Homs were bombed in retaliation for Syrian shellings of Israeli settlements with Soviet-built Frog-7 missiles, General Yariv tried to dispel the illusion that Israel would achieve the same victory over the Arabs it had achieved in 1967.

According to State Department spokesman Robert McClosky, there seemed to be intensive U.S.-Soviet contacts aimed at creating "a consensus" that would bring "a stop to the fighting and return a non-violent atmosphere to the area...." Nixon spoke of the American role in the Middle East as that of mediator, to "help build a lasting peace for the people in the troubled area."

OCTOBER 11

Israeli planes, tanks and infantry moved across the Golan Heights cease-fire line in the direction of Damascus. Holding a press conference at the front line, Dayan told reporters: "We are on the way to Damascus. It's 38 miles - from the Golan Heights - to Damascus and downhill all the way." Some 800 out of 1,400 Syrian tanks had been destroyed by Zahal. But while Dayan was militant, General Chaim Herzog, spokesman for Israeli military headquarters, clarified matters by saying that Israel's objective in Syria was not necessarily the Syrian capital city, but a key military center called Kantara, "which is very, very important to the Syrian military machine."

Golan was secured. The U.S. failed to send supplies, and Meir telephoned Nixon direct. While export licenses had been obtained, Israel discovered that it would have to pick up those supplies. But El Al planes could not carry all the tanks, planes and shells needed. In response to Meir's call, Nixon agreed to provide some transport facilities.

OCTOBER 12

In his public evaluation of Soviet participation in the Yom Kippur War, Kissinger claimed that the Soviet action could not be viewed as "irresponsible." The Soviet Union had trained, supplied and encouraged their Arab friends to make war against Israel, and yet Kissinger claimed they were acting responsibly?

Kissinger warned that if Soviet behavior did become "irresponsible" the U.S. would "not hesitate to take a firm stand." Possibly by "irresponsible" Kissinger could have meant Soviet intervention with nuclear weapons or Soviet troops. He said that he feared the Middle East might "become in time what the Balkans were in Europe before 1914." This was a phrase and historical reference that

Nixon and his people repeatedly made. Kissinger appeared to be afraid that "the great nuclear powers" would be drawn into a fight that "they did not necessarily seek or even necessarily start." Kissinger and Nixon did not know their contemporary history. In the late 19th and early 20th centuries, the major powers had competing interests in the Balkans, but they did not go to war over the Balkans. During the first and second Balkan wars of 1912-1913, the major powers had successfully spearheaded a separation of the belligerents through peaceful negotiations. But whatever historical value Nixon's and Kissinger's analysis might have had, Kissinger was trying to make it "perfectly clear" that he and the President wished to avoid a direct U.S. - U.S.S.R. war. But was he successful? The next days of the war would provide the answer.

OCTOBER 13

After days of indecision, King Hussein sent his troops into battle against Israel. He lent his support to the very state that had tried to wipe him out in 1970. Israel had supported the U.S. effort to save Trans-Jordan, but three years later, Hussein backed Arab plans to destroy Israel. Because of this stab in the back, Israel was forced to keep forces on full alert along the frontier with Trans-Jordan, but the bridges between the two states were kept open and commerce continued to fiow. A very strange war indeed.

Israel was down to a few days worth of ammunition. According to the brothers Kalb, the Nixon Administration did not resupply Israel because it did not want to antagonize the Soviets, the Arabs or the U.S. oil lobby. But while they blamed Secretary of Defense James Schlesinger, others like Leslie H. Gelb and Tad Szulc found it to be part of Kissinger's grand strategy. Gelb, in a June 23, 1974, article in *The New York Times*, quoted Schlesinger as claiming that he had followed Kissinger's policies: "there's a difference between dragging your heels and having your shoes nailed to the floor by national policy."[28] Szulc, in *New York Magazine* went much further. It was "a White House policy direction, drafted by Kissinger" that ordered a hold on resupply operations. "The written directive was a Kissingerian masterpiece of devious diplomacy." The Pentagon was presented as the "bad guys" while the White House and the State Department were made to appear as the "good guys."[29]

Regardless as to who was responsible, for a time, Israel had been abandoned by the United States. President Nixon had failed to live up to U.S. responsibilities as a so-called "friend" of Israel, and he was prepared to gamble on Israel's possible defeat. If not for the Israeli soldiers' courage, fortitude, faith and determination, Israel would have been defeated.

All available accounts indicate that the Nixon Administration was not anxious to see Israel win another Six Day War victory and become even less dependent on the U.S. The Nixons and Kissingers preferred to see Israel lose a little and thereby become more dependent on the U.S.

By October 8, Israel's Ambassador Dinitz had informed Kissinger that friends of Israel like Senators Henry Jackson, Walter Mondale, Hubert Humphrey, Birch Bayh, Abraham Ribicoff and other leading members of Congress had volunteered to help Israel get the weapons it needed. He did not know how long Israel could keep from going public on this matter. What Kissinger and Nixon feared most of all was that Israel might go public. To keep them from doing just that, Kissinger kept in touch with Ambassador Dinitz at least "six or seven times a day" and each time he promised that the arms were forthcoming.[30] By October 9, some Congressional pressure was on, but by October 11, Israel still did not have the needed supplies. Said Dinitz to Kissinger: "If a massive American airlift to Israel does not start immediately then I'll know that the United States is reneging...and we will have to draw very serious conclusions from all this." Perhaps Dinitz meant that Israel would appeal to the American people. President Nixon was overwhelmed with the Watergate scandals, and a revelation of a Kissinger-Nixon foreign affairs double-cross might finally end the Nixon Presidency. Perhaps Dinitz meant that Israel would not listen to any further U.S. policy suggestions, perhaps he meant that Israel might use any and every weapon at its disposal?

Late Friday night, October 12, Foreign Minister Eban, accompanied by Ambassador Dinitz and Shalev, went to see Secretary Kissinger. Eban broached the supplies question to Kissinger and he heard the Secretary put the blame on "other factors in the administration" who were sabotaging President Nixon's decision. In a display of concern, Kissinger called Scowcroft, his assistant, and instructed him to verify that the C-130 transports would depart for Israel on the very next day. Kissinger then turned to the Israelis and said that if the order was not carried out, Deputy Secretary of Defense William Clements would be sent back to his home state of Texas. Kissinger used Clements as his scapegoat for the failure to resupply Israel, and apparently some leaders within the Jewish community believed him.[31]

By October 13, Israel was down to less than four days of ammunition and supplies, and on that day there began a massive airlift of supplies to Israel on American cargo planes. Golda Meir had sent Nixon a desperate message. The President also had detailed reports of the Soviet airlift to the Arabs, and he had messages from King Faisal of Saudi Arabia that if the U.S. airlifted arms to Israel, the Arabs would initiate an oil embargo. Perhaps President Nixon realized that if Israel was defeated, Soviet influence with the Arabs would inevitably increase, and so the order for the airlift to Israel on U.S. cargo planes came from President Nixon. During a meeting he held with Jewish leaders on June 4, 1974, he would declare "I gave the order to send the equipment."[32]

OCTOBER 14

On Sunday, October 14, General Sharon toured the battle area of Suez and found "the way to make the crossing." While he had been commander of the southern area during four previous years, he had foreseen the possibility of having to cross the Canal. Most of the eastern side of Suez had been protected by high and very thick earthen bank towers, but he ordered one portion to be relatively thin in case of operational needs. The weak spot had been marked by red bricks, and the bulldozers were put to work there.

OCTOBER 15

By October 15, Egypt and the Soviet Union realized their offensive in the Suez area had failed. Premier Kosygin arrived in Cairo the next day and declared that the Soviets "aimed at helping the peoples of the Arab countries liberate their lands seized by Israel." President Nixon reiterated U.S. support of free nations seeking to maintain their freedom, a policy inaugurated by President Harry S Truman in 1947, and supported by every President since that time. Nixon proclaimed America's support of "every nation in the Mideast" to help maintain its "independence and security." While he recalled that Eisenhower had sent some 3,500 Marines to save Lebanon in 1958, Secretary Kissinger claimed that the U.S. had no intention of sending any troops into the area; but if the Soviets sent in forces, it would "be a different matter."

OCTOBER 16

Israeli warships attacked Egyptian ports and radar stations including those at Alexandria, some 120 miles northwest of Cairo. In the north, Israeli forces stopped near the city of Sasa, some 22 miles from Damascus because of Soviet and American pressures.

American arms finally arrived. Israel's supplies were nearly depleated in view of the heavy fighting. Huge American cargo planes brought tanks, Phantom fighters, ammunition, even uniforms. Those planes were refueled every 15 minutes at a joint U.S.-Portuguese air base in the Azores. A Portuguese officer found that the planes had "arms, munitions and bombs - everything you need for a war." Spain, France, Germany, England and other NATO states refused to permit the Americans to use NATO bases. Apparently afraid of Arab oil blackmail, they abandoned NATO in favor of personal interests and behaved towards Israel as they had behaved toward Europe's Jews during the Holocaust.

While Egypt called for a cease-fire and withdrawal by Israeli forces from territories seized in 1967, to be followed by an international peace conference at the U.N., Sadat threatened to blow up any part of Israel with Egypt's missiles. In the meantime, the six oil-producing countries on the Persian Gulf announced a 17 percent increase in their crude oil prices, but said the move had nothing to do with the war.

Meir told her Parliament that the war would end "when we have succeeded in beating the enemy." In one of the strongest statements she made during the eleven days of the war, she observed that no proposal for a cease-fire had been made to the Israeli Government and apparently the Egyptians and Syrians had "not yet been beaten enough to evince any desire for a cease-fire." She spoke of the hundreds of Israeli soldiers killed and said that she lacked the courage to "console" their families. "They are all the sons of all of us." And while she paid tribute to the United States - "Its people and Government are dear to us," she charged that the Soviet Union was the most powerful friend of the enemy. As for the British embargo of arms, it was a "grave and disgraceful imposition" at a time when Israel was fighting for "its very life."

Melvin R. Laird, Presidential advisor and former Secretary of Defense, observed that the "disruptive" Soviet activity in the Middle East threatened the future of Soviet-American *detente*. There had been a great deal of talk regarding *detente*, said Laird, but "the only way" *detente* could be proven was "by deeds not words." The Soviets had "not been performing as though *detente* was here," according to Laird.

Not till the tenth day of the war was General Sharon given the go-ahead for expanding operations into the west bank of the Suez Canal. Crossing that Canal was no easy task. General Sharon had to reach the Canal and establish a bridgehead in one night. Sharon recalled that it had to be done "before daylight because if we lost surprise about our intentions, we no doubt would have found quite a number of tanks waiting for us on the west side." By 1 a.m., Israeli forces crossed the Canal, but they were two hours behind schedule. The paratroopers met little resistance on the western side until they tried to spread their forces in order to establish a more secure perimeter. By 6 a.m., some 13 hours after the operation had begun, the tanks of the Israeli Third Brigade were crossing the Suez Canal on rafts, and by 7:30 a.m., they were all across. They spread out to attack the surface-to-air missile sites and thereby open a safe corridor in which the Israeli Air Force could operate.

While Israeli forces moved on the western side, battles raged on the eastern bank where the Egyptians sought to close the corridor the Israelis had established. After the initial battle, one could see some two dozen burnt Israeli tanks and more than 100 Egyptian tanks. General Sharon would claim that his superiors failed to send a second armored division through the bridgehead because they felt his bridgehead had not been secure enough. It was, he said, a thirty-six hour delay. And it was costly as far as forcing the Egyptians to surrender. But after that initial delay, a second and eventually a third division were sent across. But who delayed the reinforcements? Was the delay inspired by military reasons alone or were there political and diplomatic reasons as well? According to some reports, General Sharon's Canal operations were delayed because there was still a shortage of supplies. Sharon's tanks had only two days worth of 105 mm armor-piercing shells. But once American supplies arrived in sufficient quantity, Sharon's forces were reinforced.[33] And when Israel was too successful, the U.S. and the Soviet Union put the pressure on Israel to halt its activities.

OCTOBER 17

Hundreds of Israeli and Egyptian tanks clashed for control of the eastern bank of Suez over a 107 mile front while on the western bank, an Israeli force operated successfully against the Egyptians. Israeli spokesman Herzog reported that more tanks had been used in the Israeli-Arab battles than had been used in 1942 at El Alamein. Meir revealed that "additional Arab states" were about to send their forces against Israel, and Egypt's President Sadat again threatened to use long-range missiles against "the very depths of Israel."

It was a costly war for both Israel and her enemies. By October 17, the Pentagon estimated that Israel would need some $2 billion worth of U.S. F-4 Phantoms, A-4 Skyhawks, air-to-air missiles, television guided Walleye missiles, Shrike missiles and various kinds of ammunition. It was not clear as to whether Israel could afford to pay for it all, but Congressmen and Senators like Senator Stuart Symington maintained that "if the Israelis can't pay for it, we should see they get what they need regardless."

At the White House, President Nixon met with the Foreign Ministers from Saudi Arabia, Morocco, Kuwait and promised to visit Saudi Arabia. He admitted that they had differences "with regard to the means," and with regard to "certain ends as well but the goal of a fair and just and equitable peace we all are dedicated to."

OCTOBER 18

General Elazar claimed that Israel was "now calling the tune." Israeli superiority was clear and things were "going well," but it might take time to end the war. The Israeli task force operating in Egypt had been reinforced during the night and continued to operate in the central region attacking missile and anti-aircraft sites, command posts and infantry units. Israeli fighter bombers struck deep into Egyptian territory while Israeli special forces conducted sabotage operations at Egyptian naval bases on the Mediterranean and Red Seas.

As sixty-seven U.S. Senators urged Nixon to send Israel all the Phantom jets and other arms it needed to "repel the aggressors," there were indications that the U.S. and U.S.S.R. agreed in principle that the fighting should end. Addressing a U.S. Army banquet, Secretary Kissinger indicated that there was an opportunity to settle the Arab-Israeli war, and once that was achieved a "dedicated effort" would be made to "end the conditions that produced the current conflict." He revealed that the U.S. was involved "in very serious, very open-minded consultations with many countries" to bring peace.

Great Britain tried to lead a European neutrality stance in the Yom Kippur War and it called for an international peace force which would supervise demilitarized zones. Foreign Minister Eban criticized British neutrality and British notions. After meeting with West European leaders, he advised them not "to try to write the blueprint themselves...." He attacked the British embargo on the shipment of munitions and spare parts for British made Israeli Centurion tanks. This, said Eban, had cost Britain its credibility and influence in the world and with Israel in particular. As for the idea of international guarantees, Eban cited the 1971 war between India and Pakistan as indicative of the worthlessness of such guarantees. Pakistan had been a U.N. member, it had recognition from its neighbor India, it even had the support of U.S. commitments through SEATO, but when war came "the total effect was nothing and it was the balance of forces that determined the issue." The only guarantee Israel could depend upon, said Eban, was its own strength. Moreover, the Arab willingness to negotiate would demonstrate "the psychological will to come to terms," and there had to be a "visible treaty."

OCTOBER 19

As Kissinger and Nixon explored "a new formula for ending the war," Brezhnev urged that Kissinger negotiate an end to the hostilities "that might be difficult to contain were they to continue." The Arabs were losing and they were losing badly, and the Soviets became very worried. The Soviets felt insecure because for the third war since they had supported Egypt, that country was losing to Israel. Israeli forces expanded their bridgehead on the western side of the Suez Canal. Israel captured SAM-6 missiles and transported them for American experts to examine. The fight had been hard and costly. To date, we do not have the exact figures on how many Israelis and Arabs lost their lives so that the international politicians could play their nefarious games. While Israel had succeeded in trapping Egyptian forces on the east bank, some Israeli newsmen reported that it had been "the fiercest fighting" they had "seen in four wars."

President Nixon asked Congress for $2.2 billion in emergency aid to Israel "to prevent the emergence of a substantial imbalance resulting from a large-scale resupply of Syria and Egypt by the Soviet Union.'' This would be in addition to the $825 million that the U.S. had shipped to Israel during the war. The President said that he hoped to see ''a very swift and honorable'' end to the war ''measured in days, not weeks.'' But he also thought it was necessary ''to prepare for a longer struggle.''

Soon after the President's announcement, the Arabs declared their oil embargo. For the first time, they risked their oil power in their war against Israel.

OCTOBER 20

At the Soviet Union's request, Kissinger flew to Moscow to discuss the ''means to end hostilities in the Middle East.'' After two days in Moscow, he developed a formula which he believed would be ''acceptable to all parties....''

According to the Kalb brothers, while Kissinger's plane headed towards Moscow, he received two messages. One was from the White House and the other from Saudi Arabia. The White House message gave him the ''power of attorney'' to sign agreements. The Saudi Arabian message indicated that Saudi Arabia was undertaking an oil embargo on the U.S. On October 17, the Arab oil producing states had voted to reduce their production by ten percent. On October 18, Abu Dhabi imposed its embargo, Libya joined on the 19th, Saudi Arabia on the 20th and on the 21st, Algeria and Kuwait.

An Israeli column of 12,000 men and 300 tanks fought deep in Egyptian territory, smashing through waves of Arab troops. They were within some 50 miles of Cairo. At sea, the Israeli command reported that its missile boats had bombarded Egypt's Mediterranean coast between the Nile Delta cities of Damietta and Rozetta. Israeli commandos blew up ships in the Egyptian harbor at Jardaka. In the Syrian front, the Syrian tanks had been driven further back and Israeli gunboats bombarded a bridge over the El Agrash River near Syria's Mediterranean port of Tartus.

OCTOBER 21

Kissinger and the Soviets came up with a cease-fire arrangement that would presumably lead to direct talks between Egypt and Israel. Israeli commanders estimated that in two or three days, the Israeli forces on the west and east bank of the Suez Canal would have forced Egypt to surrender, but combined U.S.S.R. and U.S. pressures on

Israel forced an end to the fighting. When Nixon sent a personal appeal to Meir for an end to the fighting, she could not turn him down since Israel had become so dependent on the U.S. Again, as in 1948-49, 1956-57, and in 1967, Israel yielded to the American pressures and it agreed to a U.S.-Soviet sponsored cease-fire resolution introduced before the Security Council on October 21, 1973, and adopted during the early morning hours of October 22. The Security Council demanded that the cease-fire become effective within 12 hours or, at the latest, by 6:52 p.m. Sinai time.

OCTOBER 22

The cease-fire was to have come into effect at sundown, 6:52 p.m. Sinai time, but the fighting continued. A few hours before the truce was to begin, Kissinger visited and talked with Israeli leaders on his way back from Moscow. Israelis wondered why their government had accepted the cease-fire: "under the cease-fire arrangements the Egyptians would still be on the east side of the Canal, why should Egypt get a single inch now that we've turned the table?" Israelis were as surprised by their government's acceptance of the cease-fire as they had been with the outbreak of hostilities on October 6.

Israel approved the cease-fire when the Security Council's resolution was linked with the provision that immediately and concurrently with the cease-fire the concerned parties would negotiate a just and durable peace in the Middle East. Egypt approved with the understanding that the U.S. and U.S.S.R. would help restore the territory taken by Israel during the 1967 war.

OCTOBER 23

The fighting did not stop. Zahal further encircled Egypt's Third Army. The possibility of a Soviet-American confrontation increased. The Soviet Union threatened intervention. U.S. officials became alarmed as the Soviets warned Israel that any fruther advance of Israeli forces on the west side of Suez would have "the gravest consequences" and they called for an immediate Israeli withdrawal to the so-called October 22 lines. The U.S. pressured Israel into permitting supplies to reach the encircled Egyptian Army. General Elazar revealed that Israel had been "compelled" to accept America's resupply plan. But what was it that compelled Israel? Was it the

Soviet threat to send in its own helicopters to resupply the Egypt-ians? Was it the American threat to send in American piloted helicopters? Was it both American and Soviet pressure? Why were the Soviets so concerned for the encircled Egyptian Army? Were there many Soviet troops there? Were there so many vital Soviet military secrets there? Was it Arab prestige or Soviet prestige that worried the Kremlin dictators?

Observers like journalist Ernest Cuneo found that U.S. diplomacy was working very much for the benefit of the Arabs. When Israel had been low on ammunition and weapons, the U.S. "hesitantly, at first and nervously to the last, parcelled out equalizing but not decisive weapons from its armory." And when Israel had the Egypt-ians and Syrians on the run "where they had either to surrender or die, the U.S. came to the rescue of those Arab states." There had been reports that the U.S. pressured Israel into accepting the second cease-fire because the Soviet Union had threatened to come to Egypt's assistance, but was that the only reason the U.S. pressured Israel? To journalist Cuneo, it seemed that Washington and Moscow had worked to keep the rulers of Egypt and Syria in power, and Israel had been prevented from winning.[34]

The brothers Kalb reported that when Kissinger had learned that fighting was still raging, he became very upset. At 3 a.m., October 23, the Soviets called to tell him that Israel had "mas-sively" violated the cease-fire. In turn, Kissinger called Israel's man in Washington. "What the hell is going on?" Dinitz replied that it was Egypt, and not Israel, that had violated the cease-fire. U.S. intelligence reports verified this, and the fact that Israel was victorious. The brothers Kalb reported that Kissinger resolved to stop Israel and save the Egyptian units surrounded in Sinai. From the very start, he had tried to prevent an Israeli victory and he continued to pursue that program. Kissinger would tell Israeli and American Jewish leaders: "Israel has had it. The Jewish State is sinking fast militarily, diplomatically, and in its standing in Con-gress and public opinion."[35] He wanted those leaders to believe this and some of them did. He warned that unless Israel relied com-pletely on his diplomacy and good offices, all would be lost. That may have been an open confession of his inner feelings, and his wishful thinking that his grand plan might succeed.

OCTOBER 24

Egypt's President Sadat called for immediate Soviet-American intervention to supervise the cease-fire they had inspired. This came only hours after the Egyptian command had announced the deterioration of Egypt's military situation. The White House rejected Sadat's request saying that the U.S. had "no intention" of sending U.S. troops to the Middle East and that it hoped "other outside powers" would likewise not "send troops to the Middle East." But the Soviet Union did not reject Egypt's request.

When the Security Council met in emergency session on October 24, to consider an Egyptian request that the U.S. and U.S.S.R. intervene, the Soviets asserted that it was time to impose sanctions against Israel, and they called on all U.N. members to break diplomatic relations and trade with Israel. The resolution that was finally passed by the Security Council called for an end to the fighting, the start of negotiations "under appropriate auspices" for a peace settlement, the dispatch of U.N. military observers to supervise the cease-fire, and the return of the belligerents to their October 22 position. But who seemed to know what those October 22 positions had been?

During the night of October 24, and early morning hours of October 25, President Nixon, Secretary Kissinger, the National Security Council and other Presidential advisors conferred on the new challenge posed by the Soviet Union. A number of Soviet transport planes and ships with Soviet troops and weapons were spotted on their way to the Middle East. Some reports indicated that the Soviets had placed nuclear weapons in Egypt for possible use against Israel. According to Admiral Elmo Zumwalt, the Soviet Navy outnumbered the U.S. Sixth Fleet by a factor of three to two, and it could have brought overwhelming air power to bear. The National Security Council advised the President to call a military alert, and the President concurred. The American alert included the 82nd Airborne Division, units of the nuclear strike force and the Strategic Air Command. While Kissinger would deny that the alert had been a "missile-type-crisis," Nixon described the events as "potentially explosive" and the "most difficult crisis" since President Kennedy's confrontation over the missiles in Cuba. Another factor that provoked the American alert was the note President Nixon received from Brezhnev, General Secretary of the Soviet Communist

Party, on October 24. Admiral Zumwalt described'the letter as "savage, even by normally harsh diplomatic standards."
"It didn't even start Dear Mr. President, it just said Mr. President." It "reminded" Zumwalt of the notes that had been sent during the Cuban missile crisis.[36] On November 28, 1973, *The Washington Post* reported that the letter to Nixon read:

> I say it straight that if the U.S. does not find it possible to act together with us in this matter, we should be faced with the necessity urgently to consider the question of taking appropriate steps unilaterally.

Senator Henry Jackson described the Brezhnev letter to Nixon as "brutal." The American response, in Nixon's own words, was "also very firm and left little to the imagination of how we would react." According to a report by Joseph Alsop, the Soviets had sent a token force into Egypt despite the American alert. On the morning of October 25, six Soviet Anto-22 transports landed in Cairo with a brigade of airborne troops. Some additional troops might also have been sent into Syria.[37]

OCTOBER 25

At the Security Council, the Soviets appeared to have gotten the President's message and they responded positively to the U.S. alert. As part of a Soviet-American compromise engineered during the "alert" crisis, the Security Council approved a resolution submitted by the non-aligned nations to ship UNEF troops to the area as a buffer between Israeli and Arab forces. The veto power nations of the Security Council were ruled out as participants. But in an obvious concession to Soviet and Egyptian demands, the United States agreed to join the Soviets in sending "civilian" observers under U.N. auspices to supervise the implementation of the cease-fire.

NOVEMBER 1

Premier Golda Meir met with President Nixon and seemed "reassured" of continued American support for Israel's security and well-being. She repeatedly and emphatically denied that Israel had been under U.S. pressure to give into Egyptian demands. But some reporters were not convinced and they asked Meir why she came to Washington to see Nixon if there had been no American pressure. To "find out that there was no pressure," she answered. Nixon had assured her that "the security and well-being of Israel" was of "major concern to the United States.[38] What really transpired in her conversation with the distraught President we may not know until some more of his documents or tapes are uncovered.

The Meir visit to Nixon was followed by many weeks of hard negotiation. While a few hundred Israeli prisoners of war would finally be released by Egypt and Syria, the Israelis would be forced by American and Soviet diplomats to withdraw from positions in Sinai, the Golan Heights and the Suez west bank in exchange for tenuous cease-fire disengagement agreements and the presence of U.N. troops.

THE SEPARATION OF FORCES IN SUEZ

After weeks of intensive negotiations, orchestrated by Secretary of State Kissinger, Israel and Egypt agreed to separate their forces along the Suez Canal area. The agreement called for the withdrawal of Israeli forces to a north-south line, roughly 15 miles east of the Suez Canal, and the thinning out of Egyptian forces on the eastern bank, with U.N. forces as a buffer between Israel and Egypt. There was a second document known as the "U.S. proposal" which defined where missiles, tanks, artillery and other weapons could be deployed in the area. In his public announcement concerning the disengagement agreement, President Nixon reiterated his theme that the Middle East was the one area where the United States and the Soviet Union could be forced into a major confrontation.

Terrence Smith, *The New York Times* correspondent, reported that Israeli officials were satisfied with the disengagement agreement, and that they were hopeful for a similar agreement with Syria. But many Israelis wondered why the Egyptians had agreed to shrink their forces on the east bank of Suez to some 30 tanks and a few thousand men. Why did Egypt agree to thin out its heavy equipment on the west side? What did the Soviets and Americans promise Egypt? What had the Israeli government promised Egypt?

Israeli officials seemed to have found some advantages to the agreement. They foresaw a more stabilized cease-fire, a militarily defensible front line, normalization of relations with Egypt, and assurances that Israeli shipping would not be interfered with at Bab el Mandab. In return, they agreed to give up positions on the west bank of Suez and to withdraw several miles into Sinai. The Israeli-

Egyptian agreement was signed by the chiefs of staff of Israel and Egypt on January 18, 1974, at Kilometer 101 in the Egyptian desert.

CONCLUSIONS

The 1973 Yom Kippur War was very costly to Israel in many ways. The most costly of all was the loss of lives and the accompanying shock to its citizenry. While cities, towns and villages were saved from attack by valiant Zahal, Israel suffered some 9,000 casualties: 3,000 dead and 6,000 wounded.

It may be that peace will one day come to Israel and its Arab neighbors, but then it may be that the 1973 Yom Kippur War only served to encourage the Arabs to continue making war. Since the Arabs enjoyed some initial successes, they may believe that next time they can destroy Israel. They may forget that much of the success which they enjoyed in October 1973 was due to the interference of the Soviet Union and the United States. Israel did not pre-empt in October, it did not destroy the Egyptian Army surrounded in Sinai, it did not take Damascus or Cairo, and it accepted the cease-fires primarily because of American pressures. While Israel's political leaders proved weak, the Israeli soldier fought as bravely as did his forefathers in previous wars and centuries. Politically, the year 1973 was very much like the year 1939, when many leaders — Jewish and non-Jewish — preferred to keep silent while the major powers sought to determine the fate of the Jewish people. But there was one major difference. In the 1930s and the 1940s, the policies pursued by the major powers resulted in the death of six million Jews in less than six years. In 1973, as in 1947-49, 1956 and 1967, there were the Israeli soldiers who fought the enemy and prevented the slaughter of Israel.

American pressure on Israel intensified from 1973 to the present. From Nixon to Ford to Carter, it has been one long and difficult history for Israel. It is a long and detailed history, filled with increasing intimidation of Israel, pressures to withdraw from Sinai, Golan, the West Bank and Gaza, and to agree to the establishment of a Palestinian state. Seldom has a President of the United States shown himself to be more involved in the affairs of the states in the Middle East than Jimmy Carter. Perhaps this big brother attitude has been due to America's ever-increasing need for Arab oil? But then it seems incredible that a resourceful and inventive American nation cannot free itself from a dependence on foreign oil. President Nixon had spoken of achieving American oil independence by 1980, but America is nowhere near that goal. What is behind this inability to act? Why must American foreign policy be determined by Arab oil? The U.S. has bent over backwards to please the Arabs. It has even given some degree of legitimacy to the Palestine Liberation Organization (P.L.O.). It has helped build a multi-billion dollar air force for Saudi Arabia and it has supplied such states as Saudi Arabia with the latest air force planes. This has been done by Jimmy Carter, the man who campaigned on a platform opposed to the proliferation of armaments. As a Presidential candidate, he spoke of the Arabs needing farms and factories, not planes and bombs. But as President, he furnished the Arabs with bases, planes and bombs. This increase in the Middle East arms race and this pressure on Israel to withdraw to pre-June 1967 frontiers has only served to acerbate tensions in the Middle East. It is doubtful that any Israeli withdrawal from Sinai, Gaza or the West Bank will bring peace to the region. (The P.L.O. — child of the Arab states — has called for the complete elimination of Israel and a return to pre-November 1947 frontiers). The pre-1967 frontiers brought no peace in 1967, how can they bring peace now?

Israel finds itself in this awkward position because since 1967 it has not clarified its position on its frontiers. Concerned with world public opinion, American opinion in particular, Israel has maintained that everything is open to negotiations. But realistically, everything cannot be open to negotiations. To survive, Israel needs defensible borders. Those frontiers of June 1967 were nothing short of suicidal. From 1973 to 1978, Israel has become more dependent on the good will of the United States. It has failed to extricate itself from the complications of America's big power empire games. Unless the past thirty years have taught Israel that it cannot afford to be dependent, and that it must foresake those of its leaders (in Israel and elsewhere) who are ready to surrender, and who suffer from ghetto complexes, Israel's future may not be as fruitful as her supporters would like it to be.

1 Interview with Deputy Consul General Abiloah, Israel Consulate, New York City; March 20, 1974.
2 Yigal Allon, *The Making of the Israeli Army*.
3 *The New York Times*, October 11, 1973.

4 London Sunday Times, *Yom Kippur War*, (New York, 1974), 107. Hereafter cited as London, *Yom Kippur War*.

5 *Ibid.*, 109.

6 S.Z. Abramov, "The Agranat Report and Its Aftermath," *Midstream*, June-July 1974, 21.

7 London, *Yom Kippur War*, 107.

8 *Ibid.*

9 Matti Golan, *The Secret Conversations of Henry Kissinger*, (New York, 1976). Hereafter cited as Golan, *Conversations*.

10 *Ibid.*

11 *The New York Times*, December 10, 1973.

12 *Ibid.*, November 12, 1973.

13 *Ibid.*, December 10, 1973.

14 *Ibid.*

15 Foy D. Kohler, Leo Goure, Mose L. Harvey, *The Soviet Union and the October 1973 Middle East War, The Implications for Detente*, (University of Miami, 1974) 48-49. Hereafter cited as Kohler, *Soviet Union*. *The New York Times*, November 17, 1973.

16 Golan, *Conversations*, 39-44.

17 *Ibid.*

18 London, *Yom Kippur War*, 124-128.

19 Tad Szulc, "Is He Indispensible? Answers to the Kissinger Riddle," *New York Magazine*, July 1, 1974. Hereafter cited as Szulc, *Indispensible Kissinger?*

20 London, *Yom Kippur War*, 127-129.

21 *The New York Times*, October 26, 1973.

22 *Ibid.*

23 Marvin Kalb and Bernard Kalb, "Twenty Days in October" *The New York Times Magazine*, June 23, 1974 8ff. Hereafter cited as Kalb, *Twenty Days*.

24 *The New York Times*, October 20, 1973; Eliezer Whartman, *The Jewish Standard*, November 1, 1973.

25 *Ibid.*

26 Golan, *Conversations*, 47-50.

27 *The New York Times*, October 10, 1973.

28 *The New York Times*, June 23, 1974.

29 Szulc, *Indispensible Kissinger?*

30 Golan, *Conversations*, 49-52.

31 *Ibid.* From Conversations with Rabbi Arthur Hertzberg, July 2, 1974.

32 *Ibid.*

33 London, *Yom Kippur War*, 327ff.

34 Ernest Cuneo, "U.S. saved Arab army from a rout," *Long Island Press*, November 9, 1973.

35 Golan, *Conversations*, 108; London, *Yom Kippur War*, 254-267, 438. From conversations with Arthur Hertzberg, July 2, 1974.

36 *Long Island Press*, July 30, 1975.

37 Joseph Alsop, "And while Washington fiddles...." *Long Island Press*, November 5, 1973.

38 *The New York Times*, November 2, 1973.

Bibliography

Papers and Private Collections

American Jewish Committee Papers, New York.
American Palestine Committee Papers, Zionist Archives, New York.
American Zionist Emergency Committee Papers, Zionist Archives, New York.
Louis D. Brandeis Papers on film, Zionist Archives, New York.
Clark Clifford Papers, Harry S Truman Library, Missouri.
Benjamin V. Cohen Papers, Zionist Archives, New York.
Jacob De Haas Papers.
Harry Friedenwald Papers, Zionist Archives, New York.
Jewish Agency Papers, Zionist Archives, New York.
Julian W. Mack Papers, Zionist Archives, New York.
Admiral William D. Leahy Papers, Library of Congress, Washington.
James G. McDonald Papers, Columbia University, New York.
Samuel I. Rosenman Papers, Harry S Truman Library, Missouri.
Charles Ross Papers, Harry S Truman Library, Missouri.
Robert Szold Papers, Zionist Archives, New York.
Harry S Truman Papers, Harry S Truman Library, Missouri.
Stephen S. Wise Papers, Brandeis University, Massachusetts.
Zionist Organization of America Papers, Zionist Archives, New York.
Zionist Archives Individual Files:
  Benjamin Akzin Papers
  David Ben Gurion Papers

126

Jacob De Haas Papers
Abba Eban Papers
Albert Einstein Papers
Eliahu Epstein Papers
Nahum Goldmann Papers
Loy Henderson Papers
Vladimir Jabotinsky Papers
Rose Jacobs Papers
Eddie Jacobson Papers
I.L. Kenan Papers
George C. Marshall Papers

Autobiographies and Personal Documentaries

Allon, Yigal, *The Making of Israel's Army* (New York, 1971).
Barkley, Alben W., *That Reminds Me* (New York, 1951).
Ben Gurion, David, *Israel: A Personal History* (New York, 1972).
Byrnes, James F., *Speaking Frankly* (New York, 1947).
_____, *All in One Lifetime* (New York, 1958).
Crossman, Richard, *Palestine Mission* (New York, 1947).
Crum, Bartley C., *Behind the Silken Curtain* (New York, 1947).
Dayan, Moshe, *Story of My Life, An Autobiography* (New York, 1976).
Eban, Abba, *My Country* (New York, 1972).
Eisenhower, Dwight D., *The White House Years, Mandate for Change 1953-1956 (New York, 1963).*
_____, *The White House Years, Waging Peace, 1956-1961* (New York, 1965).
Granados, Garcia, *The Birth of Israel: The Drama as I Saw It* (New York, 1948).
Johnson, Lyndon B., *Vantage Point* (New York, 1971).
Lie, Trygve, *In the Cause of Peace: Seven Years with the United Nations* (New York, 1954).
McDonald, James G., *My Mission in Israel* (New York, 1951).
Meir, Golda, *My Life* (New York, 1975).
Neumann, Emanuel, *In the Arena, An Autobiographical Memoir* (New York, 1976).
Peres, Simon, *David's Sling* (New York, 1970)
Polier, Justine W. and Wise, James W., *Personal Letters of Stephen S. Wise (Boston, 1956).*
Phelby, H. St. John, *Arabian Jubilee* (London, 1953).
Roosevelt, Eleanor, *This I Remember* (New York, 1949).

_____, Elliot, *As He Saw It* (New York, 1945).
_____, ed. *F.D.R., His Personal Letters, 1938-1945*, Vol. II (New York, 1950).
Rosenman, Samuel, *Working with Roosevelt* (New York, 1952).
Stettinius, Edward, *Roosevelt and the Russians* (New York, 1949).
Weizmann, Chaim, *Trial and Error* (New York, 1949).
_____, Vera, *The Impossible Takes Longer* (New York, 1968).
Welles, Sumner, *We Need Not Fail* (Boston, 1948).

Published Government Documents and Newspapers

Congressional Record, 1945-1973.
Public Papers of the Presidents:
    Harry S Truman,
    Dwight D. Eisenhower,
    John F. Kennedy,
    Lyndon B. Johnson, and
    Richard M. Nixon.
United Nations General Assembly and Security Council Official Records and Minutes.
United States Department of State, *Foreign Relations of the United States*, 1945-1949.
Chicago Tribune
Jerusalem Post
Long Island Press
The New York Times
Washington Evening Star
Washington Post

Secondary Works

Alroy, Gil Carl, *The Kissinger Experience, American Policy in the Middle East* (New York, 1975).
Bar Zohar, Michael, *Ben Gurion: The Armed Prophet* (New Jersey, 1970).
_____, *Embassies in Crisis* (New Jersey, 1970).
Bober, Arie, ed., *The Other Israel* (New York, 1972).
Brecher, Michael, *Decisions in Israel's Foreign Policy* (Yale, 1975).

Daniels, Jonathan, *The Man of Independence* (New York, 1950).
Druks, Herbert, *Harry S Truman and the Russians* (New York, 1967).
_____, *The Failure to Rescue* (New York, 1977).
Elath, Eliahu, *Israel and Elath: The Political Struggle for the Inclusion of Elath in the Jewish State* (London, 1966).
Finer, Herman, *Dulles Over Suez, The Theory and Practice of His Diplomacy* (Chicago, 1964).
Friedman, Saul S., *No Haven for the Oppressed* (Detroit, 1973).
Fuchs, Lawrence H., *The Political Behavior of American Jews* (Glencoe, Illinois, 1956).
Golan, Matti, *The Secret Conversations of Henry Kissinger* (New York 1976).
Haber, Julius, *The Odyssey of an American Zionist; A Half-Century of Zionist History* (New York, 1958).
Halperin, S., *The Political World of American Zionism* (Detroit, 1961).
Halpern, Ben, *The Idea of the Jewish State* (Cambridge, 1961).
Herzog, Chaim, *The War of Atonement* (London, 1975).
Horowitz, David, *State in the Making* (New York, 1953).

Kalb, Marvin, and Bernard Kalb, *Kissinger* (Boston, 1974).
Kohler, Foy D. et al., *The Soviet Union and the October 1973 Middle East War: The Implications for Detente* (Miami, 1974).
Kurzman, Dan, *Genesis 1948, The First Arab-Israeli War* (New York, 1970).
Lacqueur, Walter Z., *The Struggle for the Middle East: The Soviet Union in the Mediterranean, 1958-1968* (New York, 1969).
Lash, Joseph P., *Eleanor: The Years Alone* (New York, 1972).
London Sunday Times, *Yom Kippur War* (New York, 1974).
Love, Kenneth, *Suez, Twice Fought War* (New York, 1969).
Manuel, Frank E., *The Realities of American-Palestine Relations* (Washington, D.C., 1949).
O'Ballance, Edgar, *The Third Arab-Israeli War* (London, 1972).
Postal, B., and Henry Levy, *And the Hills Shouted for Joy* (New York, 1973).
Safran, Nadav, *The United States and Israel* (Harvard, 1963).
_____, *From War to War: The Arab-Israeli Confrontation, 1948-1967* (Indianapolis, 1969).
Steinberg, Alfred, *The Man from Missouri* (New York, 1962).
St. John, Robert, *Eban* (New York, 1972).

Schechtman, Joseph B., *The U.S. and the Jewish State Movement, The Crucial Decade: 1939-1949* (New York, 1966).

Thomas, Abel, *Comment Israel Fut Sauve, Les Secrets de L'expedition de Suez* (Paris, 1978).

Urofsky, Melvin, *We Are One* (New York, 1978).

INDEX

4834006